Issues in Marketing

MKTG 490-01

Heidi Thom

METROPOLITAN STATE UNIV

MARKETING

ISBN-13: 9781308283074

ISBN-10: 1308283075

Contents

Credits

HARVARD | **BUSINESS** | **SCHOOL**

9-504-016
REV: JULY 10, 2006

YOUNGME MOON

JOHN QUELCH

Starbucks: Delivering Customer Service

In late 2002, Christine Day, Starbucks' senior vice president of administration in North America, sat in the seventh-floor conference room of Starbucks' Seattle headquarters and reached for her second cup of toffee-nut latte. The handcrafted beverage—a buttery, toffee-nut flavored espresso concoction topped with whipped cream and toffee sprinkles—had become a regular afternoon indulgence for Day ever since its introduction earlier that year.

As she waited for her colleagues to join her, Day reflected on the company's recent performance. While other retailers were still reeling from the post-9/11 recession, Starbucks was enjoying its 11th consecutive year of 5% or higher comparable store sales growth, prompting its founder and chairman, Howard Schultz, to declare: "I think we've demonstrated that we are close to a recession-proof product."[1]

Day, however, was not feeling nearly as sanguine, in part because Starbucks' most recent market research had revealed some unexpected findings. "We've always taken great pride in our retail service," said Day, "but according to the data, we're not always meeting our customers' expectations in the area of customer satisfaction."

As a result of these concerns, Day and her associates had come up with a plan to invest an additional $40 million annually in the company's 4,500 stores, which would allow each store to add the equivalent of 20 hours of labor a week. "The idea is to improve speed-of-service and thereby increase customer satisfaction," said Day.

In two days, Day was due to make a final recommendation to both Schultz and Orin Smith, Starbucks' CEO, about whether the company should move forward with the plan. "The investment is the EPS [earnings per share] equivalent of almost seven cents a share," said Day. In preparation for her meeting with Schultz and Smith, Day had asked one of her associates to help her think through the implications of the plan. Day noted, "The real question is, do we believe what our customers are telling us about what constitutes 'excellent' customer service? And if we deliver it, what will the impact be on our sales and profitability?"

---

[1] Jake Batsell, "A Grande Decade for Starbucks," *The Seattle Times*, June 26, 2002.

Company Background

The story of how Howard Schultz managed to transform a commodity into an upscale cultural phenomenon has become the stuff of legends. In 1971, three coffee fanatics—Gerald Baldwin, Gordon Bowker, and Ziev Siegl—opened a small coffee shop in Seattle's Pike Place Market. The shop specialized in selling whole arabica beans to a niche market of coffee purists.

In 1982, Schultz joined the Starbucks marketing team; shortly thereafter, he traveled to Italy, where he became fascinated with Milan's coffee culture, in particular, the role the neighborhood espresso bars played in Italians' everyday social lives. Upon his return, the inspired Schultz convinced the company to set up an espresso bar in the corner of its only downtown Seattle shop. As Schultz explained, the bar became the prototype for his long-term vision:

> The idea was to create a chain of coffeehouses that would become America's "third place." At the time, most Americans had two places in their lives—home and work. But I believed that people needed another place, a place where they could go to relax and enjoy others, or just be by themselves. I envisioned a place that would be separate from home or work, a place that would mean different things to different people.

A few years later, Schultz got his chance when Starbucks' founders agreed to sell him the company. As soon as Schultz took over, he immediately began opening new stores. The stores sold whole beans and premium-priced coffee beverages by the cup and catered primarily to affluent, well-educated, white-collar patrons (skewed female) between the ages of 25 and 44. By 1992, the company had 140 such stores in the Northwest and Chicago and was successfully competing against other small-scale coffee chains such as Gloria Jean's Coffee Bean and Barnie's Coffee & Tea.

That same year, Schultz decided to take the company public. As he recalled, many Wall Street types were dubious about the idea: "They'd say, 'You mean, you're going to sell coffee for a dollar in a paper cup, with Italian names that no one in America can say? At a time in America when no one's drinking coffee? And I can get coffee at the local coffee shop or doughnut shop for 50 cents? Are you kidding me?'"[2]

Ignoring the skeptics, Schultz forged ahead with the public offering, raising $25 million in the process. The proceeds allowed Starbucks to open more stores across the nation.

By 2002, Schultz had unequivocally established Starbucks as the dominant specialty-coffee brand in North America. Sales had climbed at a compound annual growth rate (CAGR) of 40% since the company had gone public, and net earnings had risen at a CAGR of 50%. The company was now serving 20 million unique customers in well over 5,000 stores around the globe and was opening on average three new stores a day. (See **Exhibits 1–3** for company financials and store growth over time.)

What made Starbucks' success even more impressive was that the company had spent almost nothing on advertising to achieve it. North American marketing primarily consisted of point-of-sale materials and local-store marketing and was far less than the industry average. (Most fast-food chains had marketing budgets in the 3%–6% range.)

For his part, Schultz remained as chairman and chief global strategist in control of the company, handing over day-to-day operations in 2002 to CEO Orin Smith, a Harvard MBA (1967) who had joined the company in 1990.

---

[2] Batsell.

The Starbucks Value Proposition

Starbucks' brand strategy was best captured by its "live coffee" mantra, a phrase that reflected the importance the company attached to keeping the national coffee culture alive. From a retail perspective, this meant creating an "experience" around the consumption of coffee, an experience that people could weave into the fabric of their everyday lives.

There were three components to this experiential branding strategy. The first component was the coffee itself. Starbucks prided itself on offering what it believed to be the highest-quality coffee in the world, sourced from the Africa, Central and South America, and Asia-Pacific regions. To enforce its exacting coffee standards, Starbucks controlled as much of the supply chain as possible—it worked directly with growers in various countries of origin to purchase green coffee beans, it oversaw the custom-roasting process for the company's various blends and single-origin coffees, and it controlled distribution to retail stores around the world.

The second brand component was service, or what the company sometimes referred to as "customer intimacy." "Our goal is to create an uplifting experience every time you walk through our door," explained Jim Alling, Starbucks' senior vice president of North American retail. "Our most loyal customers visit us as often as 18 times a month, so it could be something as simple as recognizing you and knowing your drink or customizing your drink just the way you like it."

The third brand component was atmosphere. "People come for the coffee," explained Day, "but the ambience is what makes them want to stay." For that reason, most Starbucks had seating areas to encourage lounging and layouts that were designed to provide an upscale yet inviting environment for those who wanted to linger. "What we have built has universal appeal," remarked Schultz. "It's based on the human spirit, it's based on a sense of community, the need for people to come together."[3]

Channels of Distribution

Almost all of Starbucks' locations in North America were company-operated stores located in high-traffic, high-visibility settings such as retail centers, office buildings, and university campuses.[4] In addition to selling whole-bean coffees, these stores sold rich-brewed coffees, Italian-style espresso drinks, cold-blended beverages, and premium teas. Product mixes tended to vary depending on a store's size and location, but most stores offered a variety of pastries, sodas, and juices, along with coffee-related accessories and equipment, music CDs, games, and seasonal novelty items. (About 500 stores even carried a selection of sandwiches and salads.)

Beverages accounted for the largest percentage of sales in these stores (77%); this represented a change from 10 years earlier, when about half of store revenues had come from sales of whole-bean coffees. (See **Exhibit 4** for retail sales mix by product type; see **Exhibit 5** for a typical menu board and price list.)

Starbucks also sold coffee products through non-company-operated retail channels; these so-called "Specialty Operations" accounted for 15% of net revenues. About 27% of these revenues came from North American food-service accounts, that is, sales of whole-bean and ground coffees to hotels, airlines, restaurants, and the like. Another 18% came from domestic retail store licenses that, in

---

[3] Batsell.

[4] Starbucks had recently begun experimenting with drive-throughs. Less than 10% of its stores had drive-throughs, but in these stores, the drive-throughs accounted for 50% of all business.

North America, were only granted when there was no other way to achieve access to desirable retail space (e.g., in airports).

The remaining 55% of specialty revenues came from a variety of sources, including international licensed stores, grocery stores and warehouse clubs (Kraft Foods handled marketing and distribution for Starbucks in this channel), and online and mail-order sales. Starbucks also had a joint venture with Pepsi-Cola to distribute bottled Frappuccino beverages in North America, as well as a partnership with Dreyer's Grand Ice Cream to develop and distribute a line of premium ice creams.

Day explained the company's broad distribution strategy:

> Our philosophy is pretty straightforward—we want to reach customers where they work, travel, shop, and dine. In order to do this, we sometimes have to establish relationships with third parties that share our values and commitment to quality. This is a particularly effective way to reach newcomers with our brand. It's a lot less intimidating to buy Starbucks at a grocery store than it is to walk into one of our coffeehouses for the first time. In fact, about 40% of our new coffeehouse customers have already tried the Starbucks brand before they walk through our doors. Even something like ice cream has become an important trial vehicle for us.

Starbucks Partners

All Starbucks employees were called "partners." The company employed 60,000 partners worldwide, about 50,000 in North America. Most were hourly-wage employees (called *baristas*) who worked in Starbucks retail stores. Alling remarked, "From day one, Howard has made clear his belief that partner satisfaction leads to customer satisfaction. This belief is part of Howard's DNA, and because it's been pounded into each and every one of us, it's become part of our DNA too."

The company had a generous policy of giving health insurance and stock options to even the most entry-level partners, most of whom were between the ages of 17 and 23. Partly as a result of this, Starbucks' partner satisfaction rate consistently hovered in the 80% to 90% range, well above the industry norm,[5] and the company had recently been ranked 47th in the *Fortune* magazine list of best places to work, quite an accomplishment for a company with so many hourly-wage workers.

In addition, Starbucks had one of the lowest employee turnover rates in the industry—just 70%, compared with fast-food industry averages as high as 300%. The rate was even lower for managers, and as Alling noted, the company was always looking for ways to bring turnover down further: "Whenever we have a problem store, we almost always find either an inexperienced store manager or inexperienced baristas. Manager stability is key—it not only decreases partner turnover, but it also enables the store to do a much better job of recognizing regular customers and providing personalized service. So our goal is to make the position a lifetime job."

To this end, the company encouraged promotion from within its own ranks. About 70% of the company's store managers were ex-baristas, and about 60% of its district managers were ex-store managers. In fact, upon being hired, all senior executives had to train and succeed as baristas before being allowed to assume their positions in corporate headquarters.

---

[5] Industrywide, employee satisfaction rates tended to be in the 50% to 60% range. Source: Starbucks, 2000.

Delivering on Service

When a partner was hired to work in one of Starbucks' North American retail stores, he or she had to undergo two types of training. The first type focused on "hard skills" such as learning how to use the cash register and learning how to mix drinks. Most Starbucks beverages were handcrafted, and to ensure product quality, there was a prespecified process associated with each drink. Making an espresso beverage, for example, required seven specific steps.

The other type of training focused on "soft skills." Alling explained:

> In our training manual, we explicitly teach partners to connect with customers—to enthusiastically welcome them to the store, to establish eye contact, to smile, and to try to remember their names and orders if they're regulars. We also encourage partners to create conversations with customers using questions that require more than a yes or no answer. So for example, "I noticed you were looking at the menu board—what types of beverages do you typically enjoy?" is a good question for a partner to ask.

Starbucks' "Just Say Yes" policy empowered partners to provide the best service possible, even if it required going beyond company rules. "This means that if a customer spills a drink and asks for a refill, we'll give it to him," said Day. "Or if a customer doesn't have cash and wants to pay with a check (which we aren't supposed to accept), then we'll give her a sample drink for free. The last thing we want to do is win the argument and lose the customer."

Most barista turnover occurred within the first 90 days of employment; if a barista lasted beyond that, there was a high probability that he or she would stay for three years or more. "Our training ends up being a self-selection process," Alling said. Indeed, the ability to balance hard and soft skills required a particular type of person, and Alling believed the challenges had only grown over time:

> Back in the days when we sold mostly beans, every customer who walked in the door was a coffee connoisseur, and it was easy for baristas to engage in chitchat while ringing up a bag. Those days are long gone. Today, almost every customer orders a handcrafted beverage. If the line is stretching out the door and everyone's clamoring for their coffee fix, it's not that easy to strike up a conversation with a customer.

The complexity of the barista's job had also increased over time; making a *venti tazoberry and crème*, for instance, required 10 different steps. "It used to be that a barista could make every variation of drink we offered in half a day," Day observed. "Nowadays, given our product proliferation, it would take 16 days of eight-hour shifts. There are literally hundreds of combinations of drinks in our portfolio."

This job complexity was compounded by the fact that almost half of Starbucks' customers customized their drinks. According to Day, this created a tension between product quality and customer focus for Starbucks:

> On the one hand, we train baristas to make beverages to our preestablished quality standards—this means enforcing a consistent process that baristas can master. On the other hand, if a customer comes in and wants it their way—extra vanilla, for instance—what should we do? Our heaviest users are always the most demanding. Of course, every time we customize, we slow down the service for everyone else. We also put a lot of strain on our baristas, who are already dealing with an extraordinary number of sophisticated drinks.

One obvious solution to the problem was to hire more baristas to share the workload; however, the company had been extremely reluctant to do this in recent years, particularly given the economic downturn. Labor was already the company's largest expense item in North America (see **Exhibit 3**), and Starbucks stores tended to be located in urban areas with high wage rates. Instead, the company had focused on increasing barista efficiency by removing all non-value-added tasks, simplifying the beverage production process, and tinkering with the facility design to eliminate bottlenecks.

In addition, the company had recently begun installing automated espresso machines in its North American cafés. The *verismo* machines, which decreased the number of steps required to make an espresso beverage, reduced waste, improved consistency, and had generated an overwhelmingly positive customer and barista response.

Measuring Service Performance

Starbucks tracked service performance using a variety of metrics, including monthly status reports and self-reported checklists. The company's most prominent measurement tool was a mystery shopper program called the "Customer Snapshot." Under this program, every store was visited by an anonymous mystery shopper three times a quarter. Upon completing the visit, the shopper would rate the store on four "Basic Service" criteria:

- **Service**—Did the register partner verbally greet the customer? Did the barista and register partner make eye contact with the customer? Say thank you?

- **Cleanliness**—Was the store clean? The counters? The tables? The restrooms?

- **Product quality**—Was the order filled accurately? Was the temperature of the drink within range? Was the beverage properly presented?

- **Speed of service**—How long did the customer have to wait? The company's goal was to serve a customer within three minutes, from back-of-the-line to drink-in-hand. This benchmark was based on market research which indicated that the three-minute standard was a key component in how current Starbucks customers defined "excellent service."

In addition to Basic Service, stores were also rated on "Legendary Service," which was defined as "behavior that created a memorable experience for a customer, that inspired a customer to return often and tell a friend." Legendary Service scores were based on secret shopper observations of service attributes such as partners initiating conversations with customers, partners recognizing customers by name or drink order, and partners being responsive to service problems.

During 2002, the company's Customer Snapshot scores had increased across all stores (see **Exhibit 7**), leading Day to comment, "The Snapshot is not a perfect measurement tool, but we believe it does a good job of measuring trends over the course of a quarter. In order for a store to do well on the Snapshot, it needs to have sustainable processes in place that create a well-established pattern of doing things right so that it gets 'caught' doing things right."

Competition

In the United States, Starbucks competed against a variety of small-scale specialty coffee chains, most of which were regionally concentrated. Each tried to differentiate itself from Starbucks in a different way. For example, Minneapolis-based Caribou Coffee, which operated more than 200 stores in nine states, differentiated itself on store environment. Rather than offer an upscale, pseudo-European atmosphere, its strategy was to simulate the look and feel of an Alaskan lodge, with knotty-pine cabinetry, fireplaces, and soft seating. Another example was California-based Peet's Coffee & Tea, which operated about 70 stores in five states. More than 60% of Peet's revenues came from the sale of whole beans. Peet's strategy was to build a super-premium brand by offering the freshest coffee on the market. One of the ways it delivered on this promise was by "roasting to order," that is, by hand roasting small batches of coffee at its California plant and making sure that all of its coffee shipped within 24 hours of roasting.

Starbucks also competed against thousands of independent specialty coffee shops. Some of these independent coffee shops offered a wide range of food and beverages, including beer, wine, and liquor; others offered satellite televisions or Internet-connected computers. Still others differentiated themselves by delivering highly personalized service to an eclectic clientele.

Finally, Starbucks competed against donut and bagel chains such as Dunkin Donuts, which operated over 3,700 stores in 38 states. Dunkin Donuts attributed half of its sales to coffee and in recent years had begun offering flavored coffee and noncoffee alternatives, such as Dunkaccino (a coffee and chocolate combination available with various toppings) and Vanilla Chai (a combination of tea, vanilla, honey, and spices).

Caffeinating the World

The company's overall objective was to establish Starbucks as the "most recognized and respected brand in the world."[6] This ambitious goal required an aggressive growth strategy, and in 2002, the two biggest drivers of company growth were retail expansion and product innovation.

Retail Expansion

Starbucks already owned close to one-third of America's coffee bars, more than its next five biggest competitors combined. (By comparison, the U.S.'s second-largest player, Diedrich Coffee, operated fewer than 400 stores.) However, the company had plans to open 525 company-operated and 225 licensed North American stores in 2003, and Schultz believed that there was no reason North America could not eventually expand to at least 10,000 stores. As he put it, "These are still the early days of the company's growth."[7]

The company's optimistic growth plans were based on a number of considerations:

- First, coffee consumption was on the rise in the United States, following years of decline. More than 109 million people (about half of the U.S. population) now drank coffee every day, and an additional 52 million drank it on occasion. The market's biggest growth appeared to be among drinkers of specialty coffee,[8] and it was estimated that about one-third of all U.S. coffee consumption took place outside of the home, in places such as offices, restaurants, and coffee shops. (See **Exhibit 6**.)

---

[6] Starbucks 2002 Annual Report.

[7] Dina ElBoghdady, "Pouring It On: The Starbucks Strategy? Locations, Locations, Locations," *The Washington Post*, August 25, 2002.

[8] National Coffee Association.

- Second, there were still eight states in the United States without a single company-operated Starbucks; in fact, the company was only in 150 of the roughly 300 metropolitan statistical areas in the nation.

- Third, the company believed it was far from reaching saturation levels in many existing markets. In the Southeast, for example, there was only one store for every 110,000 people (compared with one store for every 20,000 people in the Pacific Northwest). More generally, only seven states had more than 100 Starbucks locations.

Starbucks' strategy for expanding its retail business was to open stores in new markets while geographically clustering stores in existing markets. Although the latter often resulted in significant cannibalization, the company believed that this was more than offset by the total incremental sales associated with the increased store concentration. As Schultz readily conceded, "We self-cannibalize at least a third of our stores every day."[9]

When it came to selecting new retail sites, the company considered a number of criteria, including the extent to which the demographics of the area matched the profile of the typical Starbucks drinker, the level of coffee consumption in the area, the nature and intensity of competition in the local market, and the availability of attractive real estate. Once a decision was made to move forward with a site, the company was capable of designing, permitting, constructing, and opening a new store within 16 weeks. A new store typically averaged about $610,000 in sales during its first year; same-store sales (comps) were strongest in the first three years and then continued to comp positively, consistent with the company average.

Starbucks' international expansion plans were equally ambitious. Starbucks already operated over 300 company-owned stores in the United Kingdom, Australia, and Thailand, in addition to about 900 licensed stores in various countries in Asia, Europe, the Middle East, Africa, and Latin America. (Its largest international market was Japan, with close to 400 stores.) The company's goal was to ultimately have 15,000 international stores.

Product Innovation

The second big driver of company growth was product innovation. Internally, this was considered one of the most significant factors in comparable store sales growth, particularly since Starbucks' prices had remained relatively stable in recent years. New products were launched on a regular basis; for example, Starbucks introduced at least one new hot beverage every holiday season.

The new product development process generally operated on a 12- to 18-month cycle, during which the internal research and development (R&D) team tinkered with product formulations, ran focus groups, and conducted in-store experiments and market tests. Aside from consumer acceptance, whether a product made it to market depended on a number of factors, including the extent to which the drink fit into the "ergonomic flow" of operations and the speed with which the beverage could be handcrafted. Most importantly, the success of a new beverage depended on partner acceptance. "We've learned that no matter how great a drink it is, if our partners aren't excited about it, it won't sell," said Alling.

In recent years, the company's most successful innovation had been the 1995 introduction of a coffee and non-coffee-based line of Frappuccino beverages, which had driven same-store sales primarily by boosting traffic during nonpeak hours. The bottled version of the beverage (distributed

---

[9] ElBoghdady.

by PepsiCo) had become a $400 million[10] franchise; it had managed to capture 90% of the ready-to-drink coffee category, in large part due to its appeal to non-coffee-drinking 20-somethings.

Service Innovation

In terms of nonproduct innovation, Starbucks' stored-value card (SVC) had been launched in November 2001. This prepaid, swipeable smart card—which Schultz referred to as "the most significant product introduction since Frappuccino"[11]—could be used to pay for transactions in any company-operated store in North America. Early indications of the SVC's appeal were very positive: After less than one year on the market, about 6 million cards had been issued, and initial activations and reloads had already reached $160 million in sales. In surveys, the company had learned that cardholders tended to visit Starbucks twice as often as cash customers and tended to experience reduced transaction times.

Day remarked, "We've found that a lot of the cards are being given away as gifts, and many of those gift recipients are being introduced to our brand for the first time. Not to mention the fact that the cards allow us to collect all kinds of customer-transaction data, data that we haven't even begun to do anything with yet."

The company's latest service innovation was its T-Mobile HotSpot wireless Internet service, introduced in August 2002. The service offered high-speed access to the Internet in selected Starbucks stores in the United States and Europe, starting at $49.99 a month.

Starbucks' Market Research: Trouble Brewing?

Interestingly, although Starbucks was considered one of the world's most effective marketing organizations, it lacked a strategic marketing group. In fact, the company had no chief marketing officer, and its marketing department functioned as three separate groups—a market research group that gathered and analyzed market data requested by the various business units, a category group that developed new products and managed the menu and margins, and a marketing group that developed the quarterly promotional plans.

This organizational structure forced all of Starbucks' senior executives to assume marketing-related responsibilities. As Day pointed out, "Marketing is everywhere at Starbucks—it just doesn't necessarily show up in a line item called 'marketing.' Everyone has to get involved in a collaborative marketing effort." However, the organizational structure also meant that market- and customer-related trends could sometimes be overlooked. "We tend to be great at measuring things, at collecting market data," Day noted, "but we are not very disciplined when it comes to using this data to drive decision making." She continued:

> This is exactly what started to happen a few years ago. We had evidence coming in from market research that contradicted some of the fundamental assumptions we had about our brand and our customers. The problem was that this evidence was all over the place—no one was really looking at the "big picture." As a result, it took awhile before we started to take notice.

---

[10] Refers to sales at retail. Actual revenue contribution was much lower due to the joint-venture structure.

[11] Stanley Holmes, "Starbucks' Card Smarts," *BusinessWeek*, March 18, 2002.

Starbucks' Brand Meaning

Once the team did take notice, it discovered several things. First, despite Starbucks' overwhelming presence and convenience, there was very little image or product differentiation between Starbucks and the smaller coffee chains (other than Starbucks' ubiquity) in the minds of specialty coffeehouse customers. There *was* significant differentiation, however, between Starbucks and the independent specialty coffeehouses (see **Table A** below).

Table A   Qualitative Brand Meaning: Independents vs. Starbucks

Independents:
- Social and inclusive
- Diverse and intellectual
- Artsy and funky
- Liberal and free-spirited
- Lingering encouraged
- Particularly appealing to younger coffeehouse customers
- Somewhat intimidating to older, more mainstream coffeehouse customers

Starbucks:
- Everywhere—the trend
- Good coffee on the run
- Place to meet and move on
- Convenience oriented; on the way to work
- Accessible and consistent

Source: Starbucks, based on qualitative interviews with specialty-coffeehouse customers.

More generally, the market research team discovered that Starbucks' brand image had some rough edges. The number of respondents who strongly agreed with the statement "Starbucks cares primarily about making money" was up from 53% in 2000 to 61% in 2001, while the number of respondents who strongly agreed with the statement "Starbucks cares primarily about building more stores" was up from 48% to 55%. Day noted, "It's become apparent that we need to ask ourselves, 'Are we focusing on the right things? Are we clearly communicating our value and values to our customers, instead of just our growth plans?'" (see **Table B** below).

Table B   The Top Five Attributes Consumers Associate with the Starbucks Brand

- Known for specialty/gourmet coffee (54% strongly agree)
- Widely available (43% strongly agree)
- Corporate (42% strongly agree)
- Trendy (41% strongly agree)
- Always feel welcome at Starbucks (39% strongly agree)

Source: Starbucks, based on 2002 survey.

Starbucks: Delivering Customer Service   504-016

The Changing Customer

The market research team also discovered that Starbucks' customer base was evolving. Starbucks' newer customers tended to be younger, less well-educated, and in a lower income bracket than Starbucks' more established customers. In addition, they visited the stores less frequently and had very different perceptions of the Starbucks brand compared to more established customers (see **Exhibit 8**).

Furthermore, the team learned that Starbucks' historical customer profile—the affluent, well-educated, white-collar female between the ages of 24 and 44—had expanded. For example, about half of the stores in southern California had large numbers of Hispanic customers. In Florida, the company had stores that catered primarily to Cuban-Americans.

Customer Behavior

With respect to customer behavior, the market research team discovered that, regardless of the market—urban versus rural, new versus established—customers tended to use the stores the same way. The team also learned that, although the company's most frequent customers averaged 18 visits a month, the typical customer visited just five times a month (see **Figure A** below).

Figure A   Customer Visit Frequency

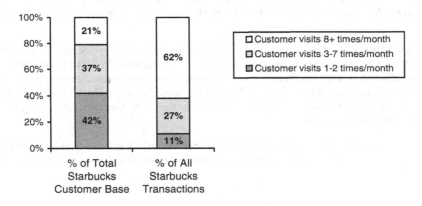

Source: Starbucks, 2002.

Measuring and Driving Customer Satisfaction

Finally, the team discovered that, despite its high Customer Snapshot scores, Starbucks was not meeting expectations in terms of customer satisfaction. The satisfaction scores were considered critical because the team also had evidence of a direct link between satisfaction level and customer loyalty (see **Exhibit 9** for customer satisfaction data).

While customer satisfaction was driven by a number of different factors (see **Exhibit 10**), Day believed that the customer satisfaction gap could primarily be attributed to a *service gap* between Starbucks scores on key attributes and customer expectations. When Starbucks had polled its customers to determine what it could do to make them feel more like valued customers, "improvements to service"—in particular, speed-of-service—had been mentioned most frequently (see **Exhibit 11** for more information).

Rediscovering the Starbucks Customer

Responding to the market research findings posed a difficult management challenge. The most controversial proposal was the one on the table before Day—it involved relaxing the labor-hour controls in the stores to add an additional 20 hours of labor, per week, per store, at a cost of an extra $40 million per year. Not surprisingly, the plan was being met with significant internal resistance. "Our CFO is understandably concerned about the potential impact on our bottom line," said Day. "Each $6 million in profit contribution translates into a penny a share. But my argument is that if we move away from seeing labor as an expense to seeing it as a customer-oriented investment, we'll see a positive return." She continued:

> We need to bring service time down to the three-minute level in all of our stores, regardless of the time of day. If we do this, we'll not only increase customer satisfaction and build stronger long-term relationships with our customers, we'll also improve our customer throughput. The goal is to move each store closer to the $20,000 level in terms of weekly sales, and I think that this plan will help us get there.

In two days, Day was scheduled to make a final recommendation to Howard Schultz and Orin Smith about whether the company should roll out the $40 million plan. In preparation for this meeting, Day had asked Alling to help her think through the implications of the plan one final time. She mused:

> We've been operating with the assumption that we do customer service well. But the reality is, we've started to lose sight of the consumer. It's amazing that this could happen to a company like us—after all, we've become one of the most prominent consumer brands in the world. For all of our focus on building the brand and introducing new products, we've simply stopped talking about the customer. We've lost the connection between satisfying our customers and growing the business.

Alling's response was simple: "We know that both Howard and Orin are totally committed to satisfying our retail customers. Our challenge is to tie customer satisfaction to the bottom line. What evidence do we have?"

504-016

Exhibit 1   Starbucks' Financials, FY 1998 to FY 2002 ($ in millions)

	FY 1998	FY 1999	FY 2000	FY 2001	FY 2002
Revenue					
Co-Owned North American	1,076.8	1,375.0	1,734.9	2,086.4	2,583.8
Co-Owned Int'l (UK, Thailand, Australia)	25.8	48.4	88.7	143.2	209.1
Total Company-Operated Retail	1,102.6	1,423.4	1,823.6	2,229.6	2,792.9
Specialty Operations	206.1	263.4	354.0	419.4	496.0
Net Revenues	**1,308.7**	**1,686.8**	**2,177.6**	**2,649.0**	**3,288.9**
Cost of Goods Sold	578.5	747.6	961.9	1,112.8	1,350.0
Gross Profit	**730.2**	**939.2**	**1,215.7**	**1,536.2**	**1,938.9**
Joint-Venture Income[a]	1.0	3.2	20.3	28.6	35.8
Expenses:					
Store Operating Expense	418.5	543.6	704.9	875.5	1,121.1
Other Operating Expense	44.5	54.6	78.4	93.3	127.2
Depreciation & Amortization Expense	72.5	97.8	130.2	163.5	205.6
General & Admin Expense	77.6	89.7	110.2	151.4	202.1
Operating Expenses	**613.1**	**785.7**	**1,023.8**	**1,283.7**	**1,656.0**
Operating Profit	**109.2**	**156.7**	**212.3**	**281.1**	**310.0**
Net Income	**68.4**	**101.7**	**94.5**	**181.2**	**215.1**
% Change in Monthly Comparable Store Sales[b]					
North America	5%	6%	9%	5%	7%
Consolidated	5%	6%	9%	5%	6%

Source: Adapted from company reports and Lehman Brothers, November 5, 2002.

[a]Includes income from various joint ventures, including Starbucks' partnership with the Pepsi-Cola Company to develop and distribute Frappuccino and with Dreyer's Grand Ice Cream to develop and distribute premium ice creams.

[b]Includes only company-operated stores open 13 months or longer.

Exhibit 2   Starbucks' Store Growth

	FY 1998	FY 1999	FY 2000	FY 2001	FY 2002
Total North America	**1,755**	**2,217**	**2,976**	**3,780**	**4,574**
Company-Operated	1,622	2,038	2,446	2,971	3,496
Licensed Stores[a]	133	179	530	809	1,078
Total International	**131**	**281**	**525**	**929**	**1,312**
Company-Operated	66	97	173	295	384
Licensed Stores	65	184	352	634	928
Total Stores	**1,886**	**2,498**	**3,501**	**4,709**	**5,886**

Source: Company reports.

[a]Includes kiosks located in grocery stores, bookstores, hotels, airports, and so on.

504-016   **Starbucks: Delivering Customer Service**

Exhibit 3   Additional Data, North American Company-Operated Stores (FY2002)

	Average
Average hourly rate with shift supervisors and hourly partners	$ 9.00
Total labor hours per week, average store	360
Average weekly store volume	$15,400
Average ticket	$ 3.85
Average daily customer count, per store	570

Source: Company reports.

Exhibit 4   Product Mix, North American Company-Operated Stores (FY2002)

	Percent of Sales
Retail Product Mix	
Coffee Beverages	77%
Food Items	13%
Whole-Bean Coffees	6%
Equipment & Accessories	4%

Source: Company reports.

Starbucks: Delivering Customer Service

504-016

Exhibit 5 Typical Menu Board and Price List for North American Company-Owned Store

Espresso Traditions	Tall	Grande	Venti		Brewed Coffee	Tall	Grande	Venti
Classic Favorites					Coffee of the Day	1.40	1.60	1.70
Toffee Nut Latte	2.95	3.50	3.80		Decaf of the Day	1.40	1.60	1.70
Vanilla Latte	2.85	3.40	3.70					
Caffe Latte	2.55	3.10	3.40		**Cold Beverages**	**Tall**	**Grande**	**Venti**
Cappuccino	2.55	3.10	3.40		Iced Caffe Latte	2.55	3.10	3.50
Caramel Macchiato	2.80	3.40	3.65		Iced Caramel Macchiato	2.80	3.40	3.80
White Chocolate Mocha	3.20	3.75	4.00		Iced Caffe Americano	1.75	2.05	3.40
Caffe Mocha	2.75	3.30	3.55					
Caffe Americano	1.75	2.05	2.40		**Coffee Alternatives**	**Tall**	**Grande**	**Venti**

Espresso	Solo	Doppio		Toffee Nut Crème	2.45	2.70	2.95
Espresso	1.45	1.75		Vanilla Crème	2.20	2.45	2.70

Caramel Apple Cider 2.45 2.70 2.95

Extras

			Hot Chocolate	2.20	2.45	2.70
Additional Espresso Shot	.55		Tazo Hot Tea	1.15	1.65	1.65
Add flavored syrup	.30		Tazo Chai	2.70	3.10	3.35

Organic milk & soy available upon request

Whole Beans: Bold	½ lb	1 lb
Our most intriguing and exotic coffees		
Gold Coast Blend	5.70	10.95
French Roast	5.20	9.95
Sumatra	5.30	10.15
Decaf Sumatra	5.60	10.65
Ethiopia Sidame	5.20	9.95
Arabian Mocha Sanani	8.30	15.95

Frappuccino	Tall	Grande	Venti		Kenya	5.30	10.15
Ice Blended Beverages					Italian Roast	5.20	9.95
Coffee	2.65	3.15	3.65		Sulawesi	6.10	11.65
Mocha	2.90	3.40	3.90				
Caramel Frappuccino	3.15	3.65	4.15		**Whole Beans: Smooth**	**½ lb**	**1 lb**
Mocha Coconut	3.15	3.65	4.15		**Richer, more flavorful coffees**		
(limited offering)					Espresso Roast	5.20	9.95

Decaf Espresso Roast 5.60 10.65

Crème Frappuccino	Tall	Grande	Venti		Yukon Blend	5.20	9.95
Ice Blended Crème					Café Verona	5.20	9.95
Toffee Nut Crème	3.15	3.65	4.15		Guatemala Antigua	5.30	10.15
Vanilla Crème	2.65	3.15	3.65		Arabian Mocha Java	6.30	11.95
Coconut Crème	3.15	3.65	4.15		Decaf Mocha Java/SWP	6.50	12.45

Tazo Tea Frappuccino	Tall	Grande	Venti		Whole Beans: Mild	½ lb	1 lb
Ice Blended Teas					**The perfect introduction to Starbucks coffees**		
Tazo Citrus	2.90	3.40	3.90		Breakfast Blend	5.20	9.95
Tazoberry	2.90	3.40	3.90		Lightnote Blend	5.20	9.95
Tazo Chai Crème	3.15	3.65	4.15		Decaf Lightnote Blend	5.60	10.65
					Colombia Narino	5.50	10.45
					House Blend	5.20	9.95
					Decaf House Blend	5.60	10.65
					Fair Trade Coffee	5.95	11.45

Source: Starbucks location: Harvard Square, Cambridge, Massachusetts, February 2003.

504-016   Starbucks: Delivering Customer Service

Exhibit 6   Total U.S. Retail Coffee Market (includes both in-home and out-of-home consumption)

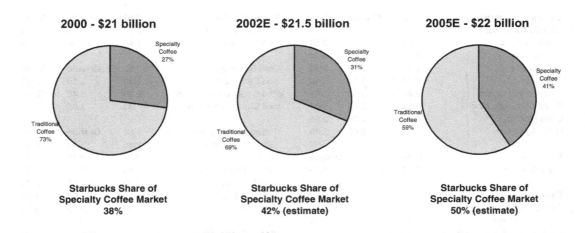

Other estimates[a] for the U.S. retail coffee market in 2002:

- In the home, specialty coffee[b] was estimated to be a $3.2 billion business, of which Starbucks was estimated to have a 4% share.

- In the food-service channel, specialty coffee was estimated to be a $5 billion business, of which Starbucks was estimated to have a 5% share.

- In grocery stores, Starbucks was estimated to have a 7.3% share in the ground-coffee category and a 21.7% share in the whole-beans category.

- It was estimated that over the next several years, the overall retail market would grow less than 1% per annum, but growth in the specialty-coffee category would be strong, with compound annual growth rate (CAGR) of 9% to 10%.

- Starbucks' U.S. business was projected to grow at a CAGR of approximately 20% top-line revenue growth.

Source: Adapted from company reports and Lehman Brothers, November 5, 2002.

[a]The value of the retail coffee market was difficult to estimate given the highly fragmented and loosely monitored nature of the market (i.e., specialty coffeehouses, restaurants, delis, kiosks, street carts, grocery and convenience stores, vending machines, etc.).

[b]Specialty coffee includes espresso, cappuccino, latte, café mocha, iced/ice-blended coffee, gourmet coffee (premium whole bean or ground), and blended coffee.

Exhibit 7   Customer Snapshot Scores (North American stores)

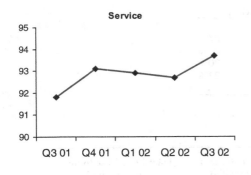

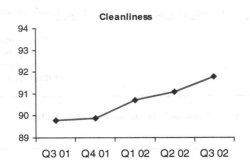

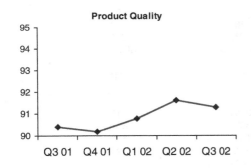

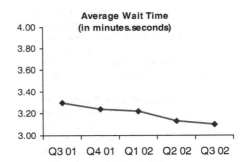

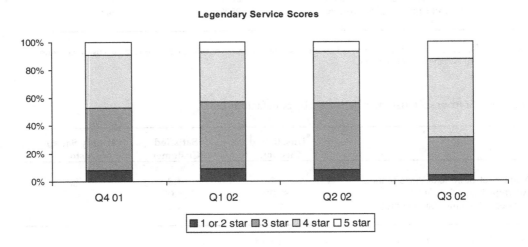

Source: Company information.

504-016

Exhibit 8   Starbucks' Customer Retention Information

% of Starbucks' customers who first started visiting Starbucks ...	
In the past year	27%
1–2 years ago	20%
2–5 years ago	30%
5 or more years ago	23%

Source: Starbucks, 2002. Based on a sample of Starbucks' 2002 customer base.

	New Customers (first visited in past year)	Established Customers (first visited 5+ years ago)
Percent female	45%	49%
Average Age	36	40
Percent with College Degree +	37%	63%
Average income	$65,000	$81,000
Average # cups of coffee/week (includes at home and away from home)	15	19
Attitudes toward Starbucks:		
High-quality brand	34%	51%
Brand I trust	30%	50%
For someone like me	15%	40%
Worth paying more for	8%	32%
Known for specialty coffee	44%	60%
Known as the coffee expert	31%	45%
Best-tasting coffee	20%	31%
Highest-quality coffee	26%	41%
Overall opinion of Starbucks	**25%**	**44%**

Source: Starbucks, 2002. "Attitudes toward Starbucks" measured according to the percent of customers who agreed with the above statements.

Exhibit 9   Starbucks' Customer Behavior, by Satisfaction Level

	Unsatisfied Customer	Satisfied Customer	Highly Satisfied Customer
Number of Starbucks Visits/Month	3.9	4.3	7.2
Average Ticket Size/Visit	$3.88	$4.06	$4.42
Average Customer Life (Years)	1.1	4.4	8.3

Source: Self-reported customer activity from Starbucks survey, 2002.

Starbucks: Delivering Customer Service   504-016

Exhibit 10   Importance Rankings of Key Attributes in Creating Customer Satisfaction

To be read: *83% of Starbucks' customers rate a clean store as being highly important (90+ on a 100-point scale) in creating customer satisfaction.*

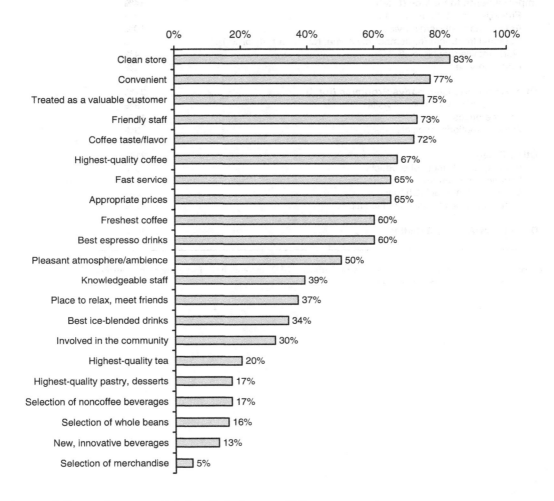

Source: Self-reported customer activity from Starbucks survey, 2002.

Exhibit 11   Factors Driving "Valued Customer" Perceptions

How could Starbucks make you feel more like a valued customer?	% Responses
Improvements to Service (total)	**34%**
Friendlier, more attentive staff	19%
Faster, more efficient service	10%
Personal treatment (remember my name, remember my order)	4%
More knowledgeable staff	4%
Better service	2%
Offer Better Prices/Incentive Programs (total)	**31%**
Free cup after x number of visits	19%
Reduce prices	11%
Offer promotions, specials	3%
Other (total)	**21%**
Better quality/Variety of products	9%
Improve atmosphere	8%
Community outreach/Charity	2%
More stores/More convenient locations	2%
Don't Know/Already Satisfied	**28%**

Source: Starbucks, 2002. Based on a survey of Starbucks' 2002 customer base, including highly satisfied, satisfied, and unsatisfied customers.

Montreaux Chocolate USA: Are Americans Ready for Healthy Dark Chocolate?

21

H A R V A R D | B U S I N E S S | S C H O O L

BRIEF CASES

9-914-501
AUGUST 4, 2013

JOHN A. QUELCH

DIANE BADAME

Montreaux Chocolate USA: Are Americans Ready for Healthy Dark Chocolate?

In October 2012, Andrea Torres, director of new product development at Montreaux Chocolate USA, was poring over data from a recent Nielsen BASES II test. Over 15 months had passed since the Consumer Foods Group (CFG) of Apollo Foods had purchased the rights to distribute Montreaux's European chocolate products in the U.S. as a means of increasing market share, in pursuit of upscale market segments. Torres was now satisfied with the research and methodology that her New Product Development (NPD) team had employed to assess market opportunity in the U.S. to date.

A board meeting was scheduled for December 10, at which Torres would be expected to make a solid, comprehensive, and compelling presentation on the status of the acquisition/assimilation of Montreaux and plans for the launch of the new product in the U.S.

David Raymond, her division manager, had committed to a set of aggressive sales forecasts that placed even greater significance on the accuracy and adequacy of the research and its application. As a result, Torres was carefully and pragmatically evaluating her options: do further product testing, launch in selected test markets, stage a regional rollout, or launch nationally?

Corporate and Company Background

Apollo Foods, a Los Angeles, California-based, global consumer packaged-goods powerhouse, offered an unrivaled portfolio of brands, manufactured confectionery, biscuits, snacks, beverages, cheese, and convenient meals, as well as an array of packaged grocery items for distribution in 170 countries. It reported 2011 revenue of $54.4 billion and net income of $3.5 billion, to which the CFG, one of four operating divisions, contributed $19.1 billion in revenue and $1.26 billion in net income. Twelve of the company's iconic brands generated revenues of over $1 billion annually and some 80 brands exceeded $100 million annually. The CFG, which was responsible for all confectionery products, managed three of those brands.

Apollo knew its consumers well and had been successfully feeding their hunger for bold flavors, easy meal solutions, and "better-for-you" offerings with more than 70 new product innovations over the past three years.

In June 2011, Apollo acquired the exclusive rights to manufacture and market Montreaux chocolate products in the U.S. from the well-known Swiss company Montreaux Chocolate Company S.A. Montreaux had long sought to expand to the U.S. but lacked the resources. Apollo was seeking a greater presence in the lucrative chocolate market and an opportunity to grow its confectionery share in the U.S., especially as it enjoyed a number-two position in the global confectionery business, largely due to products other than chocolate, such as gum and candies. This rights acquisition was the most expeditious method for both entities to achieve their goals and, given mutual reliance, offered the opportunity of an enduring and mutually rewarding relationship.

Shortly after entering into the agreement, Apollo had considered the purchase of a chocolate manufacturing facility in Pennsylvania to support the unique manufacturing processes of the Montreaux chocolate products and to serve the anticipated growth in Montreaux sales, but decided to wait until the NPD group provided a definitive launch strategy and timeline.

Apollo delegated management of the arrangement to the CFG, which formed a new division, Montreaux Chocolate USA, to operate the business. David Raymond, formerly a marketing director in the New Business Division, was named division manager. He committed to achieving aggressive goals by year-end 2015, based on Apollo's successes and marketing expertise and Montreaux's reputation as a high-quality chocolatier in Europe. The goals included:

1. National distribution of the new Montreaux product line (referring to the degree to which a given product is available for purchase or the percentage of stores carrying a given product)

2. $115 million in annual sales

3. Be in the top 25 in revenue (0.60% market share; see **Exhibit 1** for volume projections)

Montreaux personnel from Switzerland came to the U.S. and worked closely with Apollo personnel to develop Montreaux Chocolate USA's technical expertise. One engineer from Switzerland was assigned to support Torres for two years, to assist in product development and process engineering.

When Apollo first acquired the rights, it considered marketing the products through Montreaux's existing broker network but opted instead to employ Apollo's large sales force to maximize the opportunity by leveraging existing relationships. This plan of action would allow Apollo to penetrate the traditional retail channels, including "big-box" supercenters, supermarkets, drug stores, and convenience stores.

The Chocolate Confectionery Market

Chocolate is made by roasting, crushing, and refining cocoa beans. Dark chocolate is typically at least 55% cocoa; higher-quality products contain at least 70%. Milk chocolate, on the other hand, typically contains a maximum of 50% cocoa, to which milk is added. The higher concentration of cocoa in dark chocolate is the source of its claimed health benefits.

Chocolate is the most lucrative segment of the global confectionery market, accounting for 52.6% of the market's total value. In 2011, Europe captured the largest regional share of the global confectionary market at 45.2%, with the Americas following at 33.9%.[1]

The U.S. confectionery market reported total revenues of $35.648 billion in 2011, representing an annual compound growth rate of 2.8% between 2007 and 2011. Total revenue for the chocolate segment in 2011 was $17.664 billion, a 1.9% increase over 2010. The U.S. chocolate market was expected to grow almost 2% annually through 2015.[2]

Consumers' focus on fitness and health in the U.S., which sharpened over the past three decades, prompted Montreaux Chocolate USA to consider expanding its chocolate offerings to include products that featured a healthy focus. As the emphasis on healthy eating habits heightened, however, so had the number of competitors and the rate of new product introduction.

Fishers, Inc., a Dallas, Texas-based firm, was the leading global player in 2011, generating a 16.8% share of the market's value. Apollo Foods solidly held second place at 15.4%, with Swiss food giant Cornelius S.A. following at 9.1%. None of these companies, however, was the leader in the U.S. chocolate market; that honor went to Lancaster Company, with a 34.8% U.S. market share. Fishers closely followed with a 34.4% share.

The chocolate market in the U.S. is composed of seven product segments, with the top four accounting for 94.4% of market value:

1. Bar/bag/box (3.5 oz.+): $7,149 million, with 7.6% growth between 2009 and 2011

2. Seasonal chocolate: $4,407 million, with 9.9% growth

3. Bar/bag/box (less than or equal to 3.5 oz.): $3,479 million, with 18.5% growth

4. Snack-size chocolate (less than or equal to 0.6 oz.): $2,522 million, with 10.8% growth

Other segments include gift box, sugar-free, and novelty chocolate.[3]

The overall market for chocolate in the U.S. is segmented by mass market and premium, with the mass market accounting for 80.3% of sales and premium for 19.7%. The premium segment is further segmented into everyday gourmet/affordable luxury, upscale premium, and super premium, which represent 16.8%, 2.2%, and 0.7%, respectively, of total sales.[4]

Grocery, drug, and convenience stores, and Walmart, collectively sold approximately 45.3% of the chocolate candy in the U.S. in 2011. Grocery was the largest channel, accounting for 15.8% of sales followed by convenience stores at 11.7%, drug stores at 9.0%, and Walmart at 8.8%.[5]

Trends in the U.S. chocolate market in 2011 included:

1. Premium chocolate products moving to mainstream channels (i.e., supermarkets, mass merchandisers)

2. Dark chocolate sales benefiting from flavanols—antioxidants that can help to lower cholesterol and provide cardiovascular benefits

3. Low-calorie options such as reduced fat and aerated chocolate

4. Packaging going to stand-up pouches and bigger sizes that appeal to economically conscious consumers

5. New labeling with terminology emphasizing shareability, portion control, and saving a piece for later

6. Increases in pricing attributable to rising commodity costs

Consumer Attitudes and Usage

Among confection-eating adults in 2012, chocolate was consumed by 92%, who ate an average of 7.8 pieces of chocolate confectionery per month. By comparison, confection-eating children consumed less than half that amount of chocolate on average per month, although the penetration of children eating chocolate was, at 95%, slightly higher than that for adults.[6]

Chocolate consumption spanned gender, age, and household income groups, with slight variations in the formats purchased. Women were slightly more likely to eat chocolate than men (94% versus 90%), and higher-income earners were more likely to be attracted to boxed chocolates. The 45–64 age group had the highest level of per capita chocolate consumption, and that level was increasing. These consumers were prime targets for premium and specialty chocolates, and the most likely to purchase chocolate for holidays or as gifts, as well as to spend more on chocolate that they buy for others. This group was also most likely to purchase chocolate when it was on sale. Consumers increased their consumption of dark chocolate as they grew older. The "everyday sophisticates" or "bliss consumers" who bought dark chocolate were typically brand lovers, socially influential, worldly, and more willing to experiment with new foods. Montreaux Chocolate USA "loyalists" were female, aged 45–64, college educated, married with children, with household income of $50,000+, concerned about health and weight, and more likely to purchase chocolate for themselves than as a gift.

What Motivated Consumers to Purchase Chocolate?

Women who ate chocolate were more likely than men to associate it with positive experiences such as personal reward and mood enhancement. They reacted very positively to new ingredients and flavors as well as the purported benefits of improved cardiovascular fitness and lower blood pressure. In contrast, men were more focused on price and would respond positively to practical characteristics—energy boosters, quick, easy, convenient, and affordable.[7]

Convenience was a key driver of a chocolate purchase as indicated by three-quarters of consumers who purchased chocolate confectionery at supermarkets, with fairly equal percentages doing so in the candy aisle and at checkout.

Women perceived a greater distinction between premium and non-premium chocolate than did men and identified premium chocolate as a personal luxury that offered better taste and greater flavor variety. Over two-thirds of premium chocolate eaters believed it was healthier than mass-market offerings largely because lower-quality chocolate products usually contained artificial flavors, fillers, or other additives. Moreover, close to 40% of adults preferred mini and snack sizes, typically 0.25–0.60 ounces, to standard bars; given the heightened awareness of health and wellness issues, this preference may have indicated an effort to control consumption.

New Product Development at Montreaux

The NPD Group's charter was to achieve national distribution of Montreaux Chocolate USA and continue to significantly build the chocolate business in the U.S. by developing new product lines. Given the deliverable expected by senior management by year-end 2012, coupled with the company-wide focus on health and wellness, and her manager's commitments, Torres accepted NPD's recommendation to explore the growing dark chocolate category. She and her team subsequently met with Montreaux's research and development personnel, who had joined the group from Apollo, and their advertising agency to generate ideas for the new product. Out of these sessions came 45 ideas that all parties agreed merited further testing.

Montreaux decided to partner with Nielsen BASES to quantitatively assess and optimize the new dark chocolate initiative. Montreaux was keenly interested in understanding the long-term viability of the initiative, as they were going to invest significant resources in the launch and wanted the initiative to endure. BASES's extensive innovation experience had identified the 12 key things that drive successful consumer adoption of new products and empirically tied a new product's potential on these factors to the odds of in-market success (see **Exhibit 2**).

BASES, a division of the Nielsen company, a large multifaceted marketing consultancy, offers services that span the new product development process, from early idea screening through launch qualification of the final concept and product. With the help of these factors and the ability of the BASES Model to project volume potential of new products prior to launch, BASES would help Montreaux hone in on the new product opportunity and a strategy that 1) was in line with Apollo and Montreaux's **strategy** for health and wellness, 2) demonstrated strong consumer **viability**, and 3) would deliver the financial **potential** that was strong enough to meet the goals of the team. The team would be able to trace the progression of the initiative from idea to concept, to product and the BASES team would consult throughout the dark chocolate development and help Montreaux track against projections into year-one and beyond.

BASES Idea Screening Test

The first study Montreaux commissioned was a BASES Idea Screening test. BASES offers a low-cost way to quickly prioritize which new product ideas merit further development. This insight is based on performance on four of the factors that underpin the foundational strengths of an initiative and could reasonably be evaluated at the early phase of testing: Distinct Proposition, Attention Catching, Need/Desire, and Advantage (see **Exhibit 2**). From this screening Montreaux was able to narrow down the initial 45 ideas to the 12 ideas that possess the strongest potential and should be accelerated for concept development, many of which incorporated dark chocolate with fruit.

BASES Snapshot Concept Test

Montreaux understood the need to further prioritize the concept lines based on preliminary volumetric indicators as well as the feasibility of improving areas of optimization. Thus, the winning ideas moved to a BASES Snapshot concept test to identify early optimization opportunities and rough size of the price estimates prior to product development. Each idea was developed into a full concept via the addition of the concept images, messaging, varieties, and prices. A total of 200 consumers per concept were asked to evaluate the given concepts that they viewed online and to provide feedback. No actual product tasting/trial was included yet; the intent was to identify which concepts have the strongest potential to be tried by consumers in market. The BASES Snapshot identified five dark chocolate with fruit concepts that respondents considered distinct as well as attractive and relevant. However, credibility issues existed due to the unfamiliarity of the new European brand in the U.S. marketplace. With that knowledge in hand, these five "winners" were selected for further development. With the inclusion of a line-optimization analysis to better gauge the best combination of fruit flavors to include, the team confirmed that blueberry, pomegranate, and cranberry should be among the top flavors. From this testing the NPD group gave top development priority to two dark chocolate with fruit concepts, one with 70% cocoa and one with 90%.

Montreaux's R&D team then moved on to product development to find viable formulas that would meet the brand's high standards of quality and flavor at a price point consumers were willing to pay. Different types of fruit and fruit flavors, colors, and texture were developed. In addition to those identified earlier, NPD considered many other types of fruit, including goji berries, orange, acai, raspberries, and currants. At first, the number of prototypes was too large for all to be consumer-tested, so members of the project team met biweekly to taste the products and winnow the list of prototypes.

Focus Groups

Once the list of winning product formulations had been reduced to a manageable size (four in total—two with 70% cocoa and two with 90% in one of two sizes, 3.5-ounce bar or 10 squares in a 5-ounce stand-up pouch), NPD conducted eight focus groups to determine the optimal level of cocoa, reconfirm the best varieties of fruit, and refine future positioning of the line. Participants were shown headline descriptions and given samples of the four products. This qualitative research found that consumers preferred the taste of the 70% cocoa to the slightly more bitter 90% variation and also confirmed the previously identified top three flavors were also among the best tasting. The perception of healthfulness was considered the most significant difference between the new dark chocolate products and other chocolate offerings.

Marketing Issues

Aside from the product formulation, several other issues had to be addressed, including positioning, size, and packaging. Qualitative research results indicated health benefits as a potentially strong basis for positioning over taste, but NPD also noted taste was identified as an important attribute by most respondents in quantitative testing. Another positioning issue was the perception consumers should have of Montreaux Chocolate USA versus its primary competitors: Should Montreaux build upon its European brand equity or more directly tailor to the American consumer? As indicated in earlier testing, the respondents struggled with credibility issues because of the Montreaux brand name. As for size and packaging, some consumers preferred the smaller squares for portion control while others preferred the standard 3.5-ounce candy bar, and NPD needed to choose one size over the other.

Second BASES Snapshot Concept Test

Based on the research results to date, Torres decided to conduct a second BASES concept test to address these open issues. A total of 200 consumers per concept were asked to evaluate concepts that they viewed online and to provide feedback. NPD developed four refined 70% cocoa dark chocolate with fruit concepts with alternative positioning (healthy versus taste) and packaging/size (3.5-ounce bar versus squares in a 5.0-ounce stand-up pouch) for a second BASES Snapshot to determine rough revenue potential of the four optimized lines (see **Exhibit 3**).

Diagnostic information generated by the research found the 5-ounce stand-up pouch with healthy positioning to offer the greatest revenue potential, reconfirming the results of the focus group testing that found consumers respond very favorably to healthy messaging (with the smaller pieces aiding in the healthiness perception). While the 3.5-ounce bar with taste messaging was able to encourage consumers to expect to buy more often due it its smaller size, the concept was seen as less unique, thereby classifying it as a more risky proposition. Additionally, the smaller ounces and subsequent price generated less revenue than the winning pouch/health concept.

Results also found that taste was a strong secondary message that should be communicated in conjunction with the healthy positioning. The concepts were able to improve the credibility slightly by better linking the European heritage with taste. Additionally, the Snapshot suggested areas for a few potential improvements; both value and naturalness perceptions were soft (see **Exhibit 4**).

BASES II Testing

After making some minor modifications to the positioning and messaging of the product's value proposition, in August 2012, Andrea Torres decided to move forward with the BASES II testing. The methodology required contacting consumers via a proprietary Internet survey panel to gauge trial interest among a representative sample. Each respondent would be queried about their purchase interest. If they expressed the intent to buy the dark chocolate in the future, they would be shipped samples to try and then re-contacted about their product experience. Their responses would be used as inputs for the BASES volume forecasting model, including their buying intentions, intended frequency and quantity of purchase, price/value assessments, and other similar diagnostics. Results would be available within eight weeks of launching the research study.

The BASES II, the most robust concept and product evaluation offered by BASES, would allow Torres's team to evaluate the market readiness of the new dark chocolate and pinpoint potential areas of product optimization. Additionally, it would provide a one-year volume forecast by creating a simulated national-scale test market, which would allow the NPD Group to create alternative marketing scenarios by varying input parameters and then analyze the impact of these adjustments on trial rates, repeat rates, total sales volume, cannibalization, and profitability.

The team decided to test the 70% cocoa dark chocolate with fruit with healthy messaging and new stand-up pouch concept due to its heightened revenue potential, better alignment with health and wellness initiatives, and strong consumer acceptance of the proposition.

The results of the likelihood to purchase question stated that 23% of respondents would definitely buy the Montreaux dark chocolate with fruit product and 40% would probably buy the product. These ratings, along with other diagnostics, were average at best, which was somewhat unsettling to Torres.

In BASES testing, the calculations are compared to standards with which comparable products have been tested in the marketplace. This prompted the NPD team to consider testing the sensitivity of various levels of awareness and distribution low, medium, and high) to determine the degree to which first-year sales forecasts would meet or exceed the $30 million hurdle rate, assuming a retailer gross margin of 35% and manufacturer suggested retail price of $4.49 (see **Exhibit 5**). While the product results indicated the product performance was strong, the team was interested in understanding the impact if the product experience was softer as well. There were some finance team members who wanted to reduce the quality of the cocoa and understand the impact. Thus, sensitivity of the repeat rate was evaluated as well as indicated by various repeat rates for mediocre, average, and excellent product scenarios (see **Exhibit 5**). While Torres recognized that the BASES Model was much more sophisticated than NPD's immediate needs required — and could additionally provide a degree of comfort in her forecast by producing up to two years of projections for sales volume — expediency and budget constraints prevailed, as she opted to leverage commonly held forecasting assumptions in the industry to understand the rough impact of some of the key levers on year-one volumes.

914-501 | Montreaux Chocolate USA: Are Americans Ready for Healthy Dark Chocolate?

Final Steps

In preparing for the upcoming board meeting on December 10, Torres contemplated what recommendations she would bring to the meeting. She knew her boss, David Raymond, was expecting a high level of confidence in the forecasts on which he based his commitment to the three-year objectives, as did the board when evaluating the need for a new product.

Incidental at this point but nonetheless relevant to the upcoming meeting was a product name. The NPD team members had not yet made that decision. Should they continue to build brand reputation of the parent company by calling it Apollo or stay with the Montreaux name to build on the European company brand equity? Or should another brand or sub-brand name be introduced, such as Healthy Cravings, to emphasize the benefits of the dark chocolate product line with fruit? Or should the brand name be a sub-brand of Apollo?

Production facilities and processes were additional considerations. All product prototypes had been produced by Apollo's R&D technical center. Based on initial forecasts, the need for a plant was apparent but work on that project had not begun.

Torres's final decision was whether to recommend further product testing; test market the product in selected test markets; plan a regional rollout or launch nationally.

If Torres decided on a test market, the team would coordinate a full-scale, in-test market execution that entailed marketing the test product in two to four nationally representative cities through normal distribution channels. Apollo Foods would have to utilize its sales force to sell the test product to the trade and persuade retailers to carry the product in limited quantities, given it would be produced in small test batches. While this test would allow the NPD Group to holistically gauge the viability of the dark chocolate line in-market with close-to-actual market conditions prior to a wide-scale rollout, it was also the most expensive (over $3 million) and would take the longest time (one year) to obtain a proper reading of the results. This test would not only push the introduction to something beyond three years since the acquisition, but also present an element of risk as it provided the competition with an advanced notice of Montreaux Chocolate USA's new product plans and ample opportunity to buy the product off shelves, test it, and respond accordingly. Additionally, it could be very difficult to find cities that were fully representative of the U.S. consumer population.

There was an added element of complexity: The NPD team had recently learned that a competitor had also tested a dark chocolate with fruit concept and was likely not far from an introduction.

The pressure to move quickly was high.

Exhibit 1   Montreaux Chocolate USA Volume Projections

($ dollar values in millions)	2013	2014	2015
Total U.S. Market Size	$18,378	$18,745	$19,120
Montreaux Chocolate USA	$51.0	$76.0	$115.0
Montreaux U.S. Market Share	0.28%	0.41%	0.60%

Exhibit 2   Nielsen's 12 New-Product Success Factors

914-501 | Montreaux Chocolate USA: Are Americans Ready for Healthy Dark Chocolate?

Exhibit 3   Montreaux Dark Chocolate with Pomegranate Concept Board for BASES Snapshot

Introducing Montreaux Dark Chocolate with Pomegranate — A New Kind of Chocolate that Is Good for Your Health

Now you can have a delicious tasting chocolate indulgence that not only has 70% cocoa but additional natural fruit ingredients which provide antioxidants that **boost immunity to heart disease** and can **lower cholesterol**.

A 75-calorie square that cannot only satisfy that chocolate craving, but also let you feel good about it after you have thoroughly enjoyed each piece.

Flavors include pomegranate, cranberry, and blueberry.

Each 5-oz. package is priced at $4.49.

Exhibit 4   Attribute Ratings for the 5-oz. Stand-up Pouch with Healthy Messaging Concept

Product Attribute	How much would you agree with the statements made about this product? (% Agree or Strongly Agree)
Would be better for me than other chocolates	87
Would be high quality	85
Would taste great	84
Would come in varieties I like	78
Would be a good way in indulge myself	74
Would be good for any time of the day	61
Would taste better than other dark chocolates	54
Would be good for everyday use	42
Would be an all-natural snack option	38
Would be a good value	33

Exhibit 5 Montreaux Purchase Volume Estimate, Year One

Trial Purchase Rate		Repeat Rate by Product	
Definitely would buy	23%	Mediocre Product	28%
Probably would buy	40%	Average Product	33%
U.S. Households (MM)	120	Excellent Product	38%
Penetration[a]	92%	Repeat Purchase Occasions (units)	4
Marketing Plan Adjustments			
Consumer Awareness		**ACV**	
Low Support	14%	Low	60%
Medium Support	17%	Medium	65%
High Support	20%	High	79%
Pricing	$4.49	Retail Margin	35%

[a] Assumed penetration of chocolate users.

NOTE: Acceptable hurdle rate is $30MM.

All numbers are fictitious and used for illustrative purposes.

Methodology

1. Trial Rate = "Definites" * 80% + "Probables" * 30%

2. Marketing-Adjusted Trial Rate = Trial Rate * % Awareness * % ACV (distribution) * Penetration

3. Trial Households = Households x Marketing-Adjusted Trial Rate

4. Repeat Volume = Trial Households * % of Households Repurchasing * Repeat Purchase Occasions

5. Total Purchases = Trial Purchases + Repeat Purchases

6. Retail Sales Value = Retail Selling Price * Retail Sales Volume

7. Montreaux Sales Volume = Retail Sales Volume * (1 – Retailer Gross Margin – 35% or .65)

914-501 | Montreaux Chocolate USA: Are Americans Ready for Healthy Dark Chocolate?

Endnotes

[1] MarketLine, Global Confectionery, 0199-0710, November 2012, pp. 8, 10, and 12.

[2] Mintel, *Chocolate Confectionery-U.S.*, April 2012, p. 17.

[3] Ibid., p. 28.

[4] Packaged Facts, *Chocolate Candy in the U.S.*, May 2012, p. 6.

[5] Ibid., p. 10.

[6] Mintel, *Chocolate Confectionery-U.S.*, April 2012, pp. 88–89.

[7] Ibid., p. 119.

HARVARD | BUSINESS | SCHOOL

BRIEF CASES

4188

REV: NOVEMBER 30, 2011

V. KASTURI RANGAN

SUNRU YONG

Soren Chemical:
Why Is the New Swimming Pool Product Sinking?

Jen Moritz grimaced as she reviewed the February 2007 sales report for her company's new Coracle product. In September 2006, Soren Chemical had launched Coracle, a new water clarifier for use in small recreational and household swimming pools. Moritz was responsible for marketing the new clarifier, which she believed was a superior product, but the results so far were discouraging. The volume target was 50,000 gallons (100,000 units) for the first year of sales. However, through the first half of the selling season for pool chemicals, Soren had sold just 3,725 gallons, or 7,450 units.

Moritz also had responsibility for marketing Kailan MW, a clarifier used primarily in large recreational water park facilities with typical capacities of one million gallons or higher. Very small quantities of Kailan MW were sufficient to treat large volumes of water, but it was unsuitable for smaller-scale applications such as residential pools. Thus Soren Chemical had developed Coracle, targeting smaller pools with a lower volume of swimmers (known in the industry as "bather loads") and a less intense maintenance program.

In 2006, Kailan MW revenues were $6.1 million and sales were on pace for a 7% increase in 2007; it was healthy growth in a relatively mature market. Coracle had been budgeted at $1.5 million in sales for the year, but so far Soren had sold a very disappointing $111,000. The company's internal analysis estimated a $30 million market in the United States for large-scale, commercial-use clarifiers such as Kailan MW. Moritz was convinced that an even larger market existed for Coracle. She explained her challenge:

> How do we convince distributors to push Coracle and retailers to create shelf space for it? Is the product priced so that the economics are attractive to our channel partners? From the end-user perspective, most pool owners don't fully understand the safety and cost-saving benefits of Coracle. Should we invest aggressively to create greater awareness?

HBS Professor V. Kasturi Rangan and writer Sunru Yong prepared this case solely as a basis for class discussion and not as an endorsement, a source of primary data, or an illustration of effective or ineffective management. The authors thank Simon Roy of Zodiac Marine & Pool Co. and Brenda Barnicki of Eastman Chemical Co. for their valuable contributions to the development of this case. This case, though based on real events, is fictionalized, and any resemblance to actual persons or entities is coincidental. There are occasional references to actual companies in the narration.

Company Background

Timothy Soren founded the company in 1942 to sell industrial-strength cleaning solutions. In the decades since, the company had expanded its focus to include industrial chemicals for lubricants and fuels, as well as a range of chemical solutions for treating drinking water and wastewater. In 2006, the Soren Chemical product line included over 350 products, and company revenues were $450 million (see **Exhibit 1** for financial data).

Historically, Soren Chemical had concentrated on business-to-business sales and placed little emphasis on creating consumer awareness of its products. However, in 2002 the company had begun to invest selectively in developing brands for products that had potential in the consumer market. While the company had enjoyed only modest success with its branding efforts, Soren Chemical continued to invest opportunistically in products with potential beyond the traditional "B2B" core. Jen Moritz was a marketing manager in the Water Treatment Products group with responsibility for chemicals used in drinking and pool water treatment. Soren had identified in the pool water clarifier market a significant opportunity to build a consumer brand, and Moritz's role was to develop the go-to-market strategy.

Product Background

Kailan MW and Coracle are "flocculants," chemicals that cause suspended particles in liquids to agglomerate into larger, heavier particles called "flocs." They are particularly effective for microscopic particles that cannot be removed through physical filtration alone. Used under the appropriate pH, temperature, and salinity conditions, flocculating agents react with water to form insoluble hydroxides that physically trap small particles into the floc. The larger floc can then be trapped through sedimentation or filtration processes. Moritz explained:

> Flocculants can be thought of as chemical "nets" that work in conjunction with filters. To get water clean you need to get rid of particles that would otherwise pass right through filters. These particles can be as small as 0.5 microns. Only a flocculant can get something so small— the chemical "net" literally traps the little particles that filters miss, and then the net itself gets stopped by the filter.

In 2002, the Soren research and development team created the Kailan MW flocculant and found that it had application as a "clarifier" for pool water. This meant that Kailan MW was effective in dealing with oils that come from deodorant, hair spray, and lotions—which cause odors and cloudiness in water. Cloudy water is a safety hazard, obscuring pool depth for divers and making it difficult for lifeguards to see swimmers below the surface. What set Kailan MW apart from other pool clarifiers was its ability to combat organic debris. It could trap algae as well as dangerous waterborne pathogens such as E. Coli and *cryptosporidium*—a parasitic disease that normal chlorine levels do not kill. Moritz explained the importance of clarifiers as part of a pool maintenance regime:

> The layperson knows only that pools have chlorine and filters. They do not realize there is a complex system of pumps, chemicals, and UV or ozone technology used to make the water safe and clean, with minimal odor. UV systems alone, for example, cannot effectively sanitize water when there is high turbidity or cloudiness. Kailan MW captures the smallest particles and quickly reduces the cloudiness. Similarly, chlorine alone is not sufficient to make water safe because there are resistant, waterborne illnesses such as *cryptosporidium*. Any large, public pool or water park can be prone to an outbreak. That is where Kailan MW comes in.

Soren Chemical: Why is the New Swimming Pool Product Sinking? (Brief Case)

35

One gallon of Kailan MW could effectively treat approximately 500,000 gallons of water. Most competing clarifiers required daily application, but Kailan MW's advantage was its effectiveness over a longer period. Depending on the intensity of pool usage, operators could use it every other day, rather than the daily use required with similar products.

Commercial-Use Clarifiers Market

Soren Chemical estimated the 2007 U.S. market for specialty commercial-use clarifiers to be approximately $30 million, for which primary demand came from commercial pools (there are 300,000 in the U.S.) and water parks (1,000 in the U.S). Most commercial facilities must accommodate high bather loads and a disproportionate number of children, and it is imperative to maintain high levels of clarity and to protect against waterborne pathogens.

Soren Chemical sold Kailan MW for these commercial applications primarily through seven chemical formulators (see **Figure A** for an overview of the channel structure). The formulators produced or sourced the full range of pool chemicals, including chlorine tablets or liquids, cleansers, enzymes, shock treatments, and algaecides. Most products, including Kailan MW, were sold by the formulators under a private brand name.

Figure A   Pool Chemicals Channel Structure

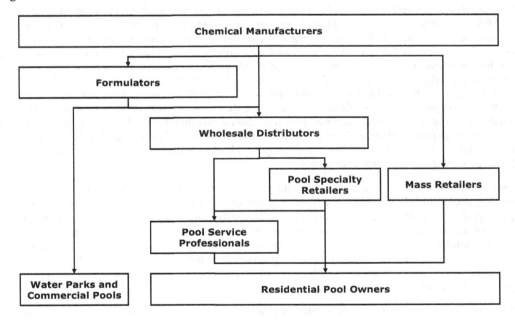

The formulators did more than simply deliver product; they typically provided a range of value-added services, such as custom blending and packaging services tailored to customer specifications. In some cases, they developed customized maintenance programs by working with water safety consultants, pump and filter manufacturers, as well as the chemical manufacturers themselves. These programs included prescribed chemical regimes tailored for different commercial applications based on typical bather loads, filter types, and other cleaning technology. The programs also accounted for regional climate conditions that affected water quality, such as pollen, insects, and pollutants. Moritz explained Soren's go-to-market strategy with Kailan MW:

> These smaller formulators are able to provide custom blends and programs, which often make them preferred suppliers for commercial usage. Soren Chemical's model does not allow us to customize for individual water parks and commercial pools. Since Kailan MW is best-suited for this market, it made sense for us to partner with the formulators.

Residential Pool Clarifiers Market

Because Kailan MW was designed for large-scale commercial facilities, Soren Chemical did not intend it for use in smaller pools for fear of misuse and potential safety risks. However, in 2005 the sales team learned that at least two of its formulators had begun marketing a diluted version of Kailan MW as a private label clarifier for the residential pool market. Moritz recognized that there was a significant, untapped market if the product could be appropriately refined for use in smaller residential pools. After several months of product development, the company unveiled a clarifier featuring chemical structure and properties similar to Kailan MW's, but designed for smaller pools, lower bather loads, and less-frequent usage. Soren named the new product "Coracle," after the traditional Welsh fishing boat that moved with the current, sweeping fish into its net.

The potential consumer market for Coracle was more fragmented than the commercial market for Kailan MW. Industry reports showed that there were nearly 9 million residential swimming pools in the United States, all of which required regular maintenance and cleaning by their owners or a professional pool service. Most pool equipment and chemical manufacturers sold via a two-step process to wholesale distributors, which then supplied specialty retailers and service professionals. Distributors typically carried tens of thousands of products from many suppliers—including the regional formulators that sold Kailan MW—and served a broad base of local retailers and pool maintenance companies. While there were a few national wholesale distributors, such as Pool Corporation, many were small regional players. Some manufacturers bypassed the wholesale distributors altogether, selling a limited range of pool products directly to Wal-Mart or "do-it-yourself" retailers such as Home Depot and Lowe's. However, this approach was costly and was used only by the largest chemical companies.

Purchasing behavior differed between professionals and consumers. The professional market, comprising pool builders, cleaning and service companies, and independent contractors, typically bought supplies from the wholesale distributors. Industry experts believed there were 40,000 to 50,000 pool contractors and service companies in the United States. Approximately 80% of consumers maintained their own pools, and they generally purchased supplies from local specialty retailers or national retailers. Whereas the critical concerns with cloudy water in the commercial market were waterborne disease and swimmer safety, the consumer market emphasized aesthetics and perceived cleanliness.

Moritz identified three leading competitors for residential pool-use clarifiers: Keystone Chemicals, Kymera, and Jackson Laboratories. She estimated that each of the companies had a 15% to 20% share of the residential pool clarifier market. Based on discussions with multiple distributors, she pieced together a product and pricing comparison (see **Table A**).

Soren Chemical: Why is the New Swimming Pool Product Sinking? (Brief Case)

37

Table A   Product Comparison

Product	Soren Chemical	Keystone Chemicals	Kymera	Jackson Labs
	Coracle	Purity	HydroPill	ClearBlu
Cost per container, retail price	**$25.00**	**$15.00**	**$3.50**	**$15.00**
Form	Liquid	Liquid	Tablet	Liquid
Gallons per container	0.50	0.25	NA	1.00
Cost per gallon, retail price	$50.00	$60.00	NA	$15.00
Cost per ounce/tablet	$0.39	$0.47	$3.50	$0.12
Ounces/tablets needed per 30K gallons	10.0	5.0	1.0	32.0
Cost per treatment, retail price	**$3.91**	**$2.34**	**$3.50**	**$3.75**
Replacement cycle (no. of monthly treatments)	2.0	4.0	2.0	4.0
Monthly cost, retail price	$7.81	$9.38	$7.00	$15.00
Average months of pool usage	5.0	5.0	5.0	5.0
Annual cost, retail price	**$39.06**	**$46.88**	**$35.00**	**$75.00**

Note: Costs are rounded.

Most service professionals considered ClearBlu to be the most effective chemical flocculant. Neither Keystone's Purity nor Kymera's HydroPill had a discernable effect in reducing the need for chlorine, shock treatments, or enzymes. In contrast, industry experts believed that ClearBlu reduced the need for other chemicals by approximately 15%, although Jackson Laboratories did not emphasize this benefit. The key disadvantage of ClearBlu was the relatively high dosage required per treatment: a quarter-gallon of product was required each week. This was higher than the dosage required with the more concentrated products of competitors, making it less convenient for pool owners and service professionals to store ClearBlu in bulk.

Marketing Strategy for Coracle

A study by Soren Chemical showed that Coracle, like Jackson Laboratories' ClearBlu, significantly boosted the efficiency of other pool chemicals by reducing the "burden" placed on chlorine. Moritz described the benefits of Coracle:

> In a typical pool, two-thirds or more of chlorine is used up oxidizing organic contaminants such as oils. This keeps the chlorine from sanitizing the water, which really defeats its primary purpose. Coracle takes care of these oils, freeing up the chlorine to serve its primary function of fighting waste. It also reduces the need for shock treatments and enzymes.[1]

The potential cost savings for pool owners could be significant. The company's research and development team estimated that Coracle reduced the need for additional chlorine, shock treatments,

---

[1] *Shock treatments* or *shock oxidizers* are heavy doses of chemicals (typically chlorine) used in conventional pools to clean out contaminants. Shock treatments may be required once a week or more, depending on the intensity of pool usage. Due to the high dosage of chemicals, shock treatments can make pools unusable for an hour or more. *Enzymes* help reduce organics and phosphates in water and are primarily intended to reduce "scum-line" formation at the edge of the pool, making it easier to clean.

4188 | Soren Chemical: Why Is the New Swimming Pool Product Sinking?

and enzymes, reducing pool owners' annual chemical costs by 20% to 30%.[2] Soren Chemical made this benefit the central thrust of its marketing message, prominently featuring the claim on the bottle.

In order to reach service professionals and specialty retailers, Soren sold Coracle through wholesale distributors. The company allowed formulators to use private branding for Kailan MW and, indeed, most opted to sell clarifiers that did not explicitly identify Kailan MW as the flocculant. However, the company decided not to allow private-label branding for Coracle, despite requests from several major wholesale distributors that marketed a number of pool chemicals under their own labels. Moritz explained how this fit into a longer-term plan:

> In keeping with Soren's new strategy to opportunistically develop consumer brands, our plan with Coracle is to make it a branded product. Our R&D pipeline includes other products, such as algae and phosphate removers that have potential in residential pools and spas. If we can build some recognition with the Coracle name, we have a platform for other products. Ideally, Coracle will become almost a consumer packaged good that pool service professionals, specialty retailers, and consumers will know and request.

The manufacturer price for a two-quart bottle of Coracle was $14.88. For most products such as chlorine, shock treatments, and enzymes, distributors typically had a 20% gross margin. However, wholesale distributors expected to maintain a 30% gross margin in selling Coracle, as it was a differentiated chemical agent. Retailers and service professionals usually took a 15% gross margin, resulting in a suggested retail price of $25 to consumers (see **Exhibit 2** for margin structure data).

The product launch in fall of 2006 was accompanied by a new website and a press release in three trade association journals targeted at pool service professionals and specialty retailers. The announcement emphasized Coracle's performance advantage in trapping dangerous waterborne pathogens such as E. Coli and *cryptosporidium*. Soren Chemical received over 2,000 inquiries from service professionals and retailers in the first three months of 2007. The company responded directly with a brochure, technical notes, and material safety data sheet.

Despite these efforts, sales through February were a dismal $111,000.

The Dilemma

Frustrated with such underperformance, Moritz reviewed her marketing plan with colleagues, noting that Soren Chemical's relative inexperience with marketing consumer-oriented brands appeared to be hindering the efforts with Coracle. One colleague questioned whether Moritz had fully accounted for competing products:

> We are new to the residential pool market and perhaps we do not fully understand the consumer. How is Coracle beneficial to them and do they understand that? They already have other choices, and Coracle is around $25, which is higher than the unit prices of competitors. I think we need to use the pricing of comparable products as our guideline.

A second colleague pointed out the challenges of selling through distributors and retailers:

> We need to be certain the economics are attractive for distributors and retailers. After all, they already carry other clarifiers. Why would they make shelf space to carry Coracle? I

---

[2] Cost savings estimates are based on chemical usage for conventional pools, which comprise over 85% of total swimming pools in the U.S. *Salt water pools* use significantly less chemicals than conventional pools, although clarifiers provide similar water safety benefits.

worry that their incentives are not totally aligned with ours. If we have room to raise prices, it might create enough margin to make this more attractive to them.

To diagnose the situation more carefully, Moritz decided to conduct a survey among the pool service professionals and specialty retailers who had made inquiries about Coracle.   The survey revealed that only 30% of the respondents recalled receiving the Coracle materials that Soren Chemical had sent in response to their inquiries. Furthermore, though Soren Chemical had passed the contact information for interested customers to the appropriate wholesale distributors, nearly 70% of respondents stated that Coracle had not been offered by their distributors. Creating greater demand from service professionals could provide a jumpstart for Coracle, but Moritz estimated that she would need a $600,000 budget to conduct a mailing campaign and to run advertising in industry publications.

Moritz also used the survey to learn from retailers and professionals about consumers' use and understanding of clarifiers (see **Exhibit 3**). Soren Chemical had priced Coracle aggressively at a $25 suggested retail price, and the estimated $39 annual cost for the average pool was lower than with most competing products. Moritz suspected that most residential pool owners simply did not realize the value of Coracle relative to other clarifiers.

The selling season for residential pool chemicals would be largely over by May. Moritz needed to reevaluate the entire go-to-market strategy. If she could identify the problem, perhaps she could partly salvage 2007 and position Coracle for a successful second year.

4188 | Soren Chemical: Why Is the New Swimming Pool Product Sinking?

Exhibit 1   Soren Financial Data ($ millions)

	2004	2005	2006
Revenue	$ 439	$ 444	$ 450
Cost of Goods Sold	335	339	345
Gross Profit	**104**	**105**	**105**
Selling, General, & Administrative Expense	29	30	31
Research & Development	8	8	9
Depreciation	15	16	15
Operating Expense	**52**	**54**	**55**
Operating Income	**52**	**51**	**50**
Provision for Tax	12	11	12
Net Income	**40**	**40**	**38**
Water Treatment Group			
Revenue	121	130	134
Gross Profit	36	39	40
Operating Income	$ 15	$ 17	$ 17

Exhibit 2   Margin Structure

	Cost per Container	Cost per Treatment
Retailer / Service Professional price	**$25.00**	**$3.91**
Retailer / Service Professional gross margin %	15%	15%
Retailer / Service Professional gross profit	$3.75	$0.59
Distributor price	**$21.25**	**$3.32**
Distributor gross margin %	30%	30%
Distributor gross profit	$6.38	$1.00
Soren Chemical price	**$14.88**	**$2.32**
Soren Chemical gross margin %	35%	35%
Soren Chemical gross profit	$5.21	$0.81

Exhibit 3   Specialty Retailer Survey, Selected Data

Annual chemical costs at retail prices, excluding clarifiers (recommended regime)	$300 average
% of consumers who understand and use clarifiers regularly	25%
Annual average cost of clarifiers at retail prices (recommended regime)	$50

HARVARD | BUSINESS | SCHOOL

9-601-163
REV: SEPTEMBER 30, 2005

SANDRA J. SUCHER

STACY E. MCMANUS

The Ritz-Carlton Hotel Company

The Master said, Govern the people by regulations, keep order among them by chastisements, and they will flee from you, and lose all self-respect. Govern them by moral force, keep order among them by ritual, and they will keep their self-respect and come to you of their own accord.

— The Analects of Confucius

James McBride, general manager of the new Ritz-Carlton in Washington, D.C., faced the largest challenge of his successful career. A proven veteran of the luxury hotel chain's march across Asia, McBride's most recent assignment was as the general manager of the 248-room Ritz-Carlton in Kuala Lumpur. Opened in 1998, the hotel was named "Best Hotel in Asia-Pacific" in the eighth *Business Traveler Asia/Pacific* magazine Travel Awards Subscribers' Survey and, for two consecutive years, "Best Business Hotel in Malaysia" by *Business Asia* and Bloomberg Television.[1] As Nikheel Advani, food and beverage services director for the Washington hotel, noted: "James is excellent—we have opened many hotels together. In the place where you didn't think that it had a chance, he made it the best hotel. That's his talent. That's what he can do really well. It's for the entrepreneurial person who wants to get involved and who thinks they can make a difference."

But this was a new situation, even for McBride. For the first time, The Ritz-Carlton was opening a hotel that was part of a multi-use facility. Owned by Millennium Partners and located in the historic Foggy Bottom district of Washington, D.C., the $225 million "hospitality complex" covered two-and-a-half acres and included 162 luxury condominiums, a 100,000 square-foot Sports Club/LA, a Splash Spa, three restaurants, 40,000 square feet of street-level restaurants and retail shops featuring the latest designs from Italy and other countries, as well as the 300-room hotel. While The Ritz-Carlton had already signed contracts to manage five other hotels for Millennium Partners, the upscale property developers had also inked deals with the Ritz's foremost competitor—the Four Seasons. Brian Collins, manager of hotels for Millennium Partners, had his own ideas about what constituted luxury service and how the hotel's general manager should approach the new-hotel opening. Under pressure from Collins, McBride was reexamining the "Seven Day Countdown," a hallmark of The Ritz-Carlton's well-defined hotel-opening process. Any changes McBride made could not only affect his company's future relationship with Millennium Partners but also the carefully guarded Ritz-Carlton brand.

---

[1] *The Mystique: The Ritz-Carlton Hotel Company, L.L.C. Employee Newsletter*, Winter 2000.

Senior Lecturer Sandra J. Sucher and Research Associate Stacy E. McManus prepared this case. HBS cases are developed solely as the basis for class discussion. Cases are not intended to serve as endorsements, sources of primary data, or illustrations of effective or ineffective management.

The Ritz-Carlton History

In 1898, Cesar Ritz saw his dream come true. Having left behind his life as a shepherd in Switzerland, he moved to Paris where he worked in some of the finest hotels and restaurants in the city before finally opening the grand hotel that bears his name. One year later, he opened London's Carlton Hotel, setting the stage for what would ultimately become The Ritz-Carlton Hotel Company.

Relying on the famous hotelier's vision of excellent personalized service that satisfied the most discerning guests, The Ritz-Carlton expanded to North America. One Great Depression and two world wars later, many of the luxurious hotels had folded. By 1983, when the Atlanta-based Johnson Company bought the North American rights to The Ritz-Carlton name, only the hotel in Boston had survived, thanks to the largesse of a wealthy property owner. From 1983 until 1997, The Ritz-Carlton expanded domestically and internationally under the Johnson Company's ownership.

In 1997, Marriott International purchased The Ritz-Carlton, which operated as a wholly owned subsidiary. By the end of 2000, The Ritz-Carlton was primarily a management company operating 38 hotels and resorts across the globe (see **Exhibit 1** for comparisons between The Ritz-Carlton and Four Seasons), with minority equity stakes in 10 properties and outright ownership of 3 hotels. The primary growth strategy for The Ritz-Carlton was to obtain management contracts for new hotels and resorts around the world (see **Figure A**).

Figure A   Ritz-Carlton New-Hotel and Resort Openings Since 1983

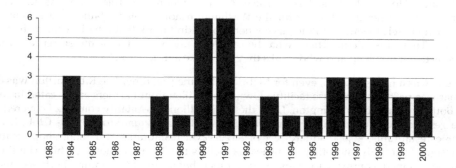

Source: Company. Number of openings represent only those that remained under the management of The Ritz-Carlton Hotel Company through 2000.

Millennium Partners Overview

Millennium Partners was a New York-based real estate development group founded in 1990 by Christopher Jeffries, Philip Aarons, and Philip Lovett. The principals initially set out to create high-end luxury apartments that would command premium prices from wealthy individuals looking for second or third homes in world-class cities. Millennium's Lincoln Square four-building complex in New York City was their first project, setting the tone for future developments. The address for celebrities such as Regis Philbin and Rosie O'Donnell also included the renowned Reebok Sports Club/NY, as well as the highest-grossing theater complex in the United States—Sony's 12-screen Lincoln Square multiplex.

Brian Collins joined Millennium Partners Management in December 1996 as their CFO, subsequently becoming the COO and a partner, as well as a principal and the president of Millennium Hospitality Partners. Collins explained how they came to be hotel owners:

> We are residential developers who ended up in the hotel business. It was not our intention to end up owning eight hotels, which is what we have under construction today—six Ritz-Carltons and two Four Seasons. Our intention was to create a base for our luxury apartments. Our vision is that apartments sell for a substantial premium if they have height, light, and views. The trick then was what to create below those apartments, which is both economical and adds to the residential experience, which also lifts it up in the air. So you try to do it with the best theater company, one who understands our vision. Then we're starting on the third floor. And you try to do it with a Sports Club. Their box, their basketball court, is about 29 feet, and that's another three stories. So if we do nothing else but have those two, we're 60 feet in the air. Washington's a bad example, because we have a 110-foot height limit. In San Francisco, the hotel is 13 stories, so the apartments are starting maybe 250 feet up in the air. And now you don't have any apartments that don't have height, light, and views.

> The other thing that helps sell residential properties is services. We said "Well, how can we solve this service problem? How do we convince people that they're going to get great, great, great service?" And Chris Jeffries hit on the idea of a luxury hotel. At the high end of the market, there's really two choices: Ritz-Carlton and Four Seasons. Ritz and Four Seasons are clearly the best hotel operators. So we've approached both, and we're doing deals with both.

Business Model

Millennium Partners was one of the several hotel owners for whom The Ritz-Carlton managed properties. The Ritz-Carlton charged management fees that were typically 3% of gross revenues, augmenting their income stream with revenues from land rent, resort timesharing, franchise fees, management incentives, and profit sharing.[2] While there were many independently owned and operated luxury hotels around the world, The Ritz-Carlton and Four Seasons were the two most internationally recognized chains serving the highest end of the market.

Two key indicators of success in the hotel industry were the average daily rate (ADR) and the revenue per available room (RevPAR; see **Exhibit 2**). While the ADR was bounded on the upper end by what the local markets would bear, RevPAR was influenced by both ADR and occupancy rates. Filling hotel rooms was crucial, and The Ritz-Carlton's general managers aggressively pursued their two main customer groups: (1) independent travelers, and (2) meeting event planners.

Guests

Independent travelers, whether for business or pleasure, were courted in a variety of ways. For instance, when McBride was the general manager of The Ritz-Carlton in Kuala Lumpur, he greeted travelers at the airport with mimosas and discount coupons presented on silver trays, serenaded them with piano concertos, and even created a hotel room in the airport, complete with an armoire, bed, television, and other accoutrements representative of the hotel's furnishings. As he prepared for the opening of the new hotel in Washington, D.C., McBride held an afternoon tea in Washington

---

[2] 1999 Marriott Lodging Annual Report.

Circle, with 100 ambassadors, prominent citizens, and members of the media enjoying the city's famed cherry blossoms as they rode to the tea in horse-drawn carriages and open trolleys.

Additionally, McBride worked to attract business travelers to The Ritz-Carlton. In Kuala Lumpur, he introduced the "Technology Butler," which comprised a staff of technicians available 24 hours a day to assist guests with computing problems and other technological difficulties. In Washington, McBride created a concierge desk at the Delta Shuttle at National Airport, implementing airport check-in procedures which provided customer convenience that outpaced the competition.

Beyond the individual initiatives of general managers, The Ritz-Carlton worldwide focused on the role of meeting events in attracting independent business travelers. The Ritz-Carlton recognized that event attendees were previewing the hotel, making every interaction they had during their stay another step in a "progressive trial." This perspective reflected the organization's recognition that their product pipeline was different from those of many others—the customers had to come to them. Because they attracted many individual guests at once, meeting event planners were seen as "the vital few" customers, representing a small number of organizations that held many large meetings in various locations around the world. These "vital few" accounted for 40% of annual sales income. According to Patrick Mene, The Ritz-Carlton's corporate vice president of quality:

> Our event business pays the mortgage. The individual traveler helps us with our profitability. The nature of our business is that a guest room and space is the most perishable product we have. An apple left unsold today can be sold tomorrow, but a room night lost today is lost forever—it's an extremely perishable product. That's why the meeting business is so desirable, because it is presold, it's contracted, and it's a growing market. It's a more controllable segment of our business.

Management Contracts

Having a strong meeting events business helped The Ritz-Carlton maintain profitability and provided property owners with acceptable returns on their investments (typically 10% to 12%, unleveraged). Nevertheless, the expense involved in operating luxury hotels (see **Exhibit 3**) sometimes strained relations between the management company and the property owners.

During the early 1980s when the hotel industry was growing at a healthy pace, traditional management contracts tended to meet the needs of both owners and operators. However, owners throughout the hotel industry had been agitating for more voice in how their properties were managed. A strong supply of management companies and a sudden decline in hotel demand led to owners gaining leverage in the management contract negotiation process,[3] a change that was facilitated by the U.S. real estate crash of the late 1980s. Many property owners lost their investments, some of whom had contracted the services of The Ritz-Carlton.

In fact, had it not been for such difficulties, The Ritz-Carlton might never have been working with Millennium Partners on the new Washington, D.C., multi-use facility. The Ritz-Carlton had previously operated a hotel in that city, but the owner, Saudi Arabian sheik Abdul Aziz bin Ibrahim al-Ibrahim, sued the company in 1995, alleging that The Ritz-Carlton operated for its own profit to the detriment of the property owner's interest. Mene provided his perspective on the situation:

---

[3] James J. Eyster, "Hotel Management Contracts in the U.S.: The Revolution Continues," *Cornell Hotel and Restaurant Administration Quarterly* 38 (3) (June 1997): 14–20.

The lawsuit involved four hotels located in New York, Washington, Aspen, and Houston, all owned by the same person. It made all the major business publications. Quite frankly, the owner just paid too much for these hotels. Our performance was noble, but he wasn't going to get his return on investment for a while, and his advisors never told him that. He just paid too much for the hotels and wanted to shift the blame to us. It took a little bit of luck, although we did walk away from him. I don't want to say the owner relations are adversarial in a typical hotel contract, but they can become strained.

Quality at The Ritz-Carlton

When Patrick Mene joined The Ritz-Carlton in 1990 as the chief quality officer, his primary mission was to integrate and prioritize the values and concepts of the Malcolm Baldrige National Quality Award criteria at all the company's hotels around the world. But before financial resources could be allocated to operational process improvements, Mene had to convince Horst Schulze, The Ritz-Carlton's president and COO since 1984 (see **Exhibit 4** for a partial organizational chart), of the importance of system and process development. As Mene recalled:

When I got here, human resources was literally the dominant function in this company. And I said, "Let's take this—we hired the right person. They're a perfect Lady and Gentleman, they went through orientation. Let's put them at the front desk. And the desk is too high to work with, and the temperature is too hot, and the computer has the wrong information coming in from another department—they can't function."

So for the next few years, Schulze would say to me, "Pat, you always try to take the human element out of it." And one day I was bold enough to say, "Yeah, you're right. Because you know what? If there were better people out there, you'd have found them by now. And I'm going to show you that we can have a ham sandwich run a Ritz-Carlton." Well, the battle lines were drawn.

While The Ritz-Carlton continued to maintain a heavy emphasis on human resources, the total quality management (TQM) philosophy began to permeate the organization. Using the Malcolm Baldrige National Quality Award criteria as a set of guidelines, Schulze and Mene focused on a variety of new activities and measures, including the cost of poor quality, continuous improvement, quality planning, benchmarking, supplier certification, and quality audits. Other programs were designed to meet specific customer needs, such as safety protocols to protect the children of guests, and the Service Quality Indicators (SQIs) were established (see **Exhibit 5**).

One of the components of the SQIs involved guest-recognition procedures. As an owner, Collins wanted to see that improved for the new Washington, D.C. hotel:

I pushed James [McBride] to hire more people than The Ritz-Carlton staffing plan would lead them to hire in Guest Recognition. I think it's the single most important thing we can do. If a guest came in, got what they wanted, and were recognized, all of a sudden that creates a sticky relationship. It's all about organizing your thoughts and creating processes to recognize the person coming in to the hotel.

So after a certain number of visits to one of our Ritz hotels, guests will get a monogrammed pillowcase. It will be in their room so that when they check in, they'll go to their room and say, "Oh, my pillow's here. Isn't that great!" And no one expects it, so the first time, it's like "Wow!" We're doing something different from The Ritz-Carlton standard—we're clearly exceeding the standard. But they don't force every owner to abide by that higher standard, so sometimes there is friction about raising the standard outside of the Ritz program. I want to rethink it, rethink it all from start to finish. And it just drives them crazy.

Even so, the standards The Ritz-Carlton had already established were recognized as outstanding (see **Exhibit 6**). The company applied for and won the Baldrige Award in 1992, becoming the first organization in the hospitality industry to receive the coveted honor. The extensive feedback report from the Baldrige evaluators identified an additional 75 areas for improvement and, using those suggestions as action guidelines, The Ritz-Carlton applied for and won the award again in 1999, becoming only the second American company to earn the distinction more than once. Schulze expressed his belief in TQM:

Winning this award confirms that quality is not a short-term approach to doing business. Instead, it is a road map that allows us to achieve the highest customer and employee satisfaction in the industry. Continuous improvement is absolutely critical. If managers are not improving something every day, they are on a death path. Companies that are plateauing because of traditional management will die. Period.

Human Resources at The Ritz-Carlton

The way The Ritz-Carlton viewed its employees was a distinguishing hallmark of the organization. According to Leonardo Inghilleri, the corporate vice president of human resources:

We respect our employees. The issue of respect is a philosophical issue that is driven by our leadership. You have to have a passion for people. If you have an accounting approach to human resources, then you're bound to fail. If you look at an employee and say, "He's a full-time equivalent, he's an FTE; he is eight hours of labor," I think that's immoral. An employee is a human being who doesn't only fulfill a function but should also have a purpose. So a successful business is one that is capable of enlisting an employee not only for his muscles and his labor, but also for his brain, his heart, and his soul.

In hotels that were up and running for at least a year, The Ritz-Carlton's annual turnover rate was only 20%, compared with the hotel industry average of 100%, while new hotels experienced turnover rates between 20% and 25% during the first 60 days. Inghilleri believed that it was his company's deep respect for its employees that led to their satisfaction with and commitment to the organization. The Ritz-Carlton was so intent on treating their employees well that a "Day 21" event was held as a process check three weeks after any new hire's start date. During that session, the company assessed the degree to which it had lived up to the promises it made to its employees during orientation and initial training.

One of those promises included opportunities for career advancement, which were abundant at The Ritz-Carlton. Corporatewide, 25% of the organization's managerial workforce began their careers at The Ritz-Carlton as hourly employees, such as dishwasher, housekeeper, and restaurant server, or as hourly supervisors. For example, Kate Monahan advanced from reservations manager to general manager: "Fourteen years ago, I set out to find a job—but what I began was a career. Along the way, The Ritz-Carlton has nurtured and maximized my talent."[4] Similarly, Alex Garza began as a line cook and eventually became an executive sous chef. As Garza stated:

---

[4] As quoted in *The Mystique: The Ritz-Carlton Hotel Company, L.L.C. Employee Newsletter*, Winter 2000.

The Ritz Carlton has been a kind and generous employer. I have always been treated fairly and as a gentleman, with the utmost respect for my talents. Because this organization cared about my career path and my goals from the outset, and because it has demonstrated respect for my talents along the way, I have been able to grow. At The Ritz-Carlton, opportunities for advancement are everywhere. It's up to you how far you want to go.[5]

Through the extensive formal and informal training offered by The Ritz-Carlton (see **Exhibit 7**), employees were prepared to fulfill their current obligations and to accept positions of greater responsibility and accountability in the future. Employees with advancement ambitions were encouraged to cross-train and learn about as many different aspects of the organization as possible.

Performance at The Ritz-Carlton was not only assessed against the established Service Quality Indicators but also managed by the employees themselves. As Inghilleri explained:

We have created an environment where there is no fear of retribution, an environment where employees understand that their responsibility is not only to fulfill functions but also to have a purpose. One of their purposes is to improve the system. When you have a good person and you create a good environment for that person, he or she doesn't come to work to do a bad job—they come to work to do a good job. So it doesn't make sense for us to punish people if something goes wrong.

We verify whether the problem is a lack of resources or a lack of training, and then we address the problem accordingly. Our employees are taught from the very beginning that there is nothing more exciting than fixing a mistake or defect. They want to see the defects, they want to find out what they are, because once that's known, they can be corrected. We've never had a problem with people hiding mistakes, because it's just not the culture of the company.

In addition to employees monitoring their own performance, individuals were recognized for outstanding work in a variety of ways, including small awards given within departments, as well as larger rewards that occurred at the hotel level. For instance, each year every hotel identified members of a "Five-Star Team," each of whom received five complimentary nights at a Ritz-Carlton hotel of their choice, $500 to spend, and round-trip airfare for two.

The Ritz-Carlton Hotel-Opening Process

According to one manager at The Ritz-Carlton, "Running an ongoing operation is a very different thing from opening a new hotel. They are actually two different core competencies." The processes and focus of activity for creating new hotels were two-pronged: one dealing with the development of the site itself, the other involving the human resources processes necessary to get the hotel up and running. The entire hotel development process was assessed against Performance Quality Indicators (PQIs; see **Exhibit 8**), the 10 defects identified by The Ritz-Carlton as most likely to lead to problems with both quality and financial performance. Mene noted that while developing a hotel was "a very complex, cross-departmental, cross-functional, cross-company process in general, the PQI represents the key pitfalls."

---

[5] Ibid.

The Property

Many decisions had to be made when The Ritz-Carlton set out to open any new hotel, including site selection, concept/new-product development, feasibility studies, and management contract negotiation. When explaining the importance of site selection, Mene succinctly stated, "I mean, let's just put it this way. What if we build a 300-room hotel where there's no hotel needed at all? You're dead. It's done. It's over." The new Washington, D.C., location was desirable because of its proximity to several sites of interest, such as the White House and Capitol Hill, Embassy Row, and the Foggy Bottom Historic District; Washington's status as a global destination; and the potentially strong clientele base of foreign diplomats and local residents.

Feasibility studies were conducted that identified the primary target customers, as well as their wants, needs, and expectations. Then financial evaluations determined the cost to the developer and the price charged to the customers—two key issues for consideration prior to moving ahead. All of this activity was carried out in a time-pressured environment. As Mene noted: "Late feasibility studies are deadly, because the developers may be talking to our foremost competitor and they may be faster with the feasibility study than us. We're really in competition here." Once a contract had been signed, construction on the new property began, with both The Ritz-Carlton and the owners participating in decisions regarding the development.

Market Customization

In addition to general concerns about the property, The Ritz-Carlton had to customize each hotel to meet local market demands. As McBride elaborated, "There is great credence given to the importance of taking local information and then adapting to it. That's what we learned in Asia, and that's what I've been doing for six years—adapting locally to do business there." One of the adaptations that occurred at the new Washington, D. C., hotel involved the Secret Service walking the site and discussing the planning of entrances and exits with the developers. Given the likelihood of foreign diplomats and ambassadors being guests of the hotel, security design became an issue of potential international importance.

Innovations for the savvy guests the hotel expected to attract took more creative turns as well. For example, McBride planned to link services provided by the hotel's main restaurant, Kobalt, to the Internet. Customers would be able to go to KobaltExpress.com where they could order their menus ahead of time and select the table they would like to reserve, while Kobalt@home.com would allow condominium residents to order meals to their suites. McBride also planned to incorporate an exhibition kitchen into the Kobalt, explaining, "This restaurant is not going to be a traditional Ritz-Carlton restaurant."

That was not the only aspect of the new hotel that broke with tradition; according to Collins, Millennium Partners took an active role in defining the interior spaces: "We picked out all the art. You won't see one English hunting scene in this hotel—and it's been painful for the Ritz. Their competition is the Four Seasons, and the Ritz has been resting on its laurels—'We're an English kind of hotel'—and that just is not going to get it done in the 2000s. It's just not what people want."

Millennium Partners' choices of artwork resulted in a collection valued at about $2 million, including hand-blown glass designs by Seattle's Dale Chihuly. The highest thread-count Egyptian cotton fabric was used for all the linens, down comforters covered each bed, and the bathrooms were tiled in beige and white marble. Further breaking with traditional Ritz-Carlton designs, the property contained a 34,000-square-foot Japanese garden complete with a cascading waterfall, bamboo plants, and willow trees.

Staffing the New Hotel

The property owners had the right to approve the individuals nominated by The Ritz-Carlton for three executive positions: general manager, director of marketing, and controller. Once McBride was selected as the general manager, he was instrumental in choosing the additional members of the hotel's executive committee, almost all of whom had experience at other Ritz-Carlton properties. These leaders were in place about two and a half months prior to the scheduled hotel opening.

The executive committee then selected their functional managers, who were, in turn, primarily responsible for hiring line-staff members. In hotels that were already operating, the selection process was often inverted, with the line staff selecting their leaders from a pool of candidates. Similarly, line-staff applicants typically were selected and trained by relevant team members, but for new-hotel openings, the process was much more structured and hierarchical.

Millennium Partners' concerns regarding the hotel's new staff centered on the distinction between effectively opening and running a hotel, as Collins explained:

I've got to tell you that I love James McBride. James McBride is just fabulous. He's successfully opened up lots of Ritz-Carltons. But a year from now? We'll have done it for 365 days, and the edge will be off a little bit. The problem in the hotel business is that you have to fill it up every single day. So somehow you have to put your game face on and be 99% every single day. But even then, that means you're ticking off a customer every single day. I don't know how you do it a year out, two years out, five years out. I don't know how you keep it sharp. And that's the trick.

As The Ritz-Carlton's president and COO, Schulze was all too aware of the difficulty of keeping it sharp. Having worked his way from a waiters' apprentice and dishwasher to the top of one of the world's best hotel companies, Schulze knew firsthand how hard it could be for employees to maintain their motivation to deliver exceptional service to customers every single day, and how difficult it could be for managers and leaders to keep morale up after the fanfare of a new-hotel opening. To help minimize failures in service delivery, Schulze focused on key human resource practices, particularly employee recruitment, selection, and training.

Personnel recruitment   A wide variety of tools was used to attract applicants for the staff positions at the new hotel. McBride was active in the recruitment process, dining at The Ritz-Carlton's arch-competition and giving deserving servers cards that read "The Service You Just Provided Was First Class!" on one side and contained job-application information on the other. More traditionally, targeted ads for food and beverage personnel were run in the newspapers of major cites (e.g., New York and San Francisco), while the community within Washington, D.C., also provided fertile ground for potential employees. The first hospitality high school in the United States was located in the area, and The Ritz-Carlton also interviewed individuals in welfare-to-work programs.

For positions that required technical expertise or high-level service delivery, individuals with significant prior experience were hired. For more entry–level positions, novices to the hospitality industry were acceptable. As Marie Minarich, the hotel's human resources director, said: "If they have the talent, and if they want to serve people, we can train them. We can teach them the skills they need to perform any number of different functions. As long as we make sure that we choose people who fit our culture, we can work with them."

Ritz-Carlton job fair   A two-day mass recruitment occurred on August 22 and 23, 2000, from 8:00 a.m. to 8:00 p.m. and was billed as a "Ritz-Carlton Job Fair." Individuals who had previously applied, as well as those who had not, were invited to the site (still under construction at the time) where they went through the selection procedure. Throughout both days, the goal was to treat applicants to a personal demonstration of the service-oriented culture that made The Ritz-Carlton famous.

At the Foggy Bottom Metro stop, three uniformed Ritz-Carlton representatives stood by large placards advertising the job fair, ready to provide directions to the site. The path between the Metro and The Ritz-Carlton was marked with cobalt blue ribbons. Just outside the entrance to the building, applicants arrived at the "Warm Welcome" station, where they were greeted at the door by one of several employees who wished them luck and escorted them past a violinist into the lower level of the hotel where the meeting rooms had been outfitted. Greeters then escorted applicants to the registration area, where Claude Hedspeth provided entertainment with his electric piano. Despite performing for over 25 years, this was the first time he had ever played at a job fair.

In the waiting room, where beverages and snacks were available, a Ritz-Carlton video was running in which Schulze talked about his early days as a dishwasher and other Ritz-Carlton employees described their experiences at the company. After the applicants provided basic employment information, they went through a standardized selection procedure that first involved the administration of a screening questionnaire. Those who made it past the initial screening proceeded on to a professionally developed and validated structured interview. Each individual was then personally escorted to "Fond Farewell," where they were thanked for applying, given miniature Ritz-Carlton chocolates, and escorted out of the building.

By 2:00 p.m. on the first day, over 400 individuals had been through the process, and everyone, from McBride on down, pitched in to serve as escorts, paperwork runners, and interviewers—and that was before the local news media aired a blitz of stories about the hotel. Over 10 years had passed since a luxury hotel opened in Washington, D.C., and television crews swarmed the job fair.

The aftershock was felt on the second day, when 1,500 individuals showed up to compete for positions. By the time all was said and done, 2,300 people had been through the selection process in 24 hours, while another 1,700 had already completed the application process prior to the job fair. These were impressive numbers, especially given the local unemployment rate of only 5.4%.[6] About 400 people were eventually hired, which made getting a job at The Ritz-Carlton about as likely as being accepted as a Harvard undergraduate.

Individuals who did not make the cut were treated the same as everyone else during the job fair, as Inghilleri explained:

> We try to make sure that those we don't hire are treated really well. They may also be sons and daughters of our customers, we don't know. So why would I mistreat them? If someone is not hired and we just disregard them, what does that accomplish? You create someone in the community who looks at you and says, "Those guys are morons. They are arrogant imbeciles who don't understand who I am, who didn't value me as a person." We don't want that.

For the new hires, The Ritz-Carlton utilized a pre-employment call-back process to reduce the attrition that often occurred during the lag between the job offer and the start date (see **Exhibit 9**). During this phase of the employer-employee relationship, new employees were treated as customers with their own unique set of needs, and the hotel's managers were accountable for their satisfaction.

---

[6] "Local Area Unemployment Statistics for the District of Columbia," Bureau of Labor Statistics, August 2000, http://146.142.4.24/cgi-bin/surveymost.

The Ritz-Carlton Hotel Company

601-163

The Seven Day Countdown

The Seven Day Countdown was a result of the evolution and refinement of the hotel-opening process, which became more solidified in the late 1980s to early 1990s when the hotel chain was opening many new properties. Standardization brought greater efficiency and relieved some of the burden placed on new managers and leaders responsible for ultimately running the hotel.

Individuals' first encounter with the organization as employees occurred over a month after they had been hired, when they showed up for the beginning of the Seven Day Countdown prior to the opening of the hotel. The first two days were devoted entirely to orienting employees to The Ritz-Carlton culture and values, while the remaining five days involved more specific skills training and trial runs of service delivery. According to Collins, ensuring that everything was perfect on opening day would be a challenge:

> There's all this construction activity going on around here, finishing floors, testing the fire-alarm system. And they have 400 people they have to convert to Ritz-Carlton employees in the next seven days. They have to be trained and dipped into the culture of The Ritz-Carlton so that on day one when Ms. Jones checks in, she's getting a true Ritz experience. Seven days. I've told James I just don't know if that's enough time.

To help the new staff members navigate their way through the demanding Seven Day Countdown, The Ritz-Carlton provided each of them with a "Paper Palm" (see **Exhibit 10**). Inghilleri explained the rationale behind the countdown's organization:

> We have a very slow orientation process that aligns the worker with the mission of the company. The reality is that, as an adult, you only change your behavior from a significant emotional experience, and otherwise you don't change. When you hire someone to start a new job, it is a significant emotional experience for them, so they will be attentive and receptive to behavioral changes.

> But the size of the window of opportunity that the company has to drive home new concepts is limited. So if you waste the first few hours of the first few days discussing anything other than values, you're wasting your opportunity. That is why in our orientation, the first thing we do is discuss values.

Day One: Staff Orientation

On the first day of the countdown, new employees joined other members of their divisions outside the hotel for what can only be described as a pep rally. Carrying signs and chanting ("House-keep-ing, House-keep-ing"), each division vied to be the loudest, most enthusiastic group of new employees. The kitchen staff had the advantage, banging out Stomp-worthy rhythms on their pots and pans. At least one manager made a brave attempt at turning cartwheels along the covered drive leading to the entrance of the new hotel, while others ran from one end of the line to the other, encouraging more cheering.

After several rounds of "the wave" and chants of "D-C-Ritz, D-C-Ritz," the staff members eventually entered the building. As they slowly wound their way downstairs toward the ballrooms where their first training sessions would occur, the employees heard the sound of enthusiastic applause. It was coming from the hotel's managers, who lined both sides of the curved marble staircase. Many times over, each employee was sincerely welcomed as a new member of The Ritz-

Carlton family by the scores of managers who smiled warmly and said, "We're so happy you're here," "Welcome," "I'm so glad you've come."

Once inside, everyone gathered in the largest ballroom, where video cameras were hooked up to big-screen TVs providing a simulcast of all the activity. Recordings of Sting singing "We're starting up a brand new day . . .," Queen's "Another One Bites the Dust," and the always-popular "We Are the Champions" played as the employees congregated. Once everyone was present, McBride introduced the hotel's leadership team, followed by The Ritz-Carlton trainers, who had come from 23 different countries around the world for the countdown. Individuals chosen as trainers represented the "best of the best" of The Ritz-Carlton worldwide—all of whom had significant experience opening new Ritz-Carlton properties. Introductions progressed to the corporate steering committee and then to the Millennium Partners representatives. Finally, McBride spoke to the assembled, immediately conveying to them the importance of opening the hotel at the highest level possible from day one: "We will open as the finest hotel in Washington, D.C., without a doubt. We are like Olympic gymnasts who have been training for years and years. Then it all comes down to the big performance, and the gymnasts must stick their landings—otherwise, they are not excellent. We will stick our landings. We will be excellent."

Next, the new employees watched a video in which Schulze and others described the hotel company's history, philosophy, and values, followed by a second tape that described The Ritz-Carlton's milestones, including awards they had won and new hotels they had opened. The applause and cheering were abundant when The Ritz-Carlton, Washington, D.C., appeared on the screen.

Schulze's Address

Schulze entered the room to a standing ovation as Queen's "We Will Rock You" blared over the speaker system. Addressing all the employees of the new hotel, Schulze explained his philosophy of being a high-quality service organization:

> You are not servants. We are not servants. Our profession is service. We are Ladies and Gentlemen, just as the guests are, who we respect as Ladies and Gentlemen. We are Ladies and Gentlemen and should be respected as such.

> I grew up in a small village in Germany. When I was 11 or 12, I decided to go into the hotel business—I don't know why. My mother told me, "The guests are very fine, important people." To me, they looked like gods. My knees were shaking. I was scared. As the months went by, I never stopped seeing them as fine ladies and gentlemen. But when our maitre d' dressed impeccably, and spoke to them in fluent English, German, or Spanish, it became clear that he was as much a gentleman as anyone in the room, because of the excellence with which he did his job. If we do what we do right, we become as important as they are.

This was how the employees learned the genesis of The Ritz-Carlton motto ("We Are Ladies and Gentlemen Serving Ladies and Gentlemen"). According to Schulze, the motto was a "deeply believed feeling and demand on the organization," a promise by the organization that everyone would be respected as a lady or a gentleman. It was also a demand on all employees, especially managers and leaders.

The Gold Standards

The motto was one part of The Gold Standards (see **Exhibit 11**), implemented by Schulze in the mid-1980s. These standards included The Credo, The Three Steps of Service, The Motto, The

Employee Promise, and The Twenty Basics, which were designed to focus employees on the core company values. According to Schulze, when an employee adopted The Credo, that person was in effect saying, "This is who I am from now on." Different aspects of The Gold Standards were reinforced daily through departmental "lineups," which occurred at the beginning of every shift, in every hotel, around the world. They were used to reinforce the company's philosophy and to repeat the foundation of the business over and over in order to build the habits necessary for employees to deliver the highest level of service demanded by The Ritz-Carlton. Inghilleri explained the importance of the daily lineups:

> Our employees are on the front lines. They are always on the battlefield. So you've got to nourish them on a daily basis—you have to heal the wounds of being on the battlefield daily. Otherwise, they'll forget the real reasons they are there.

> After cleaning 16 rooms to our standards, you are exhausted. You come back to work the following morning, and if I don't remind you that the customers are important, that being nice to them is critical, that eliminating defects is paramount, that the genuine care of the customer is crucial, well, then you'll forget. You'll think that you just come to work to clean rooms.

Service Philosophy

Complementing the concepts in The Gold Standards, Schulze further explained The Ritz-Carlton philosophy to the new employees during their first day of orientation: "We are not in the hotel business. The hotel business is about selling rooms, selling food, selling the bar. We do those things incidentally, but our business is service. We charge for service. Our commitment to our customers is excellence in service. Service is our profession." During his address to the employees on their first official day as members of The Ritz-Carlton, Schulze also set the stage for how they could expect to be treated within the organization:

> For these next few days, we will orient you to who we are—our heart, our soul, our goals, our vision, our dreams—so you can join us, and not just work for us. You have a right to know who we are and what we think. You have a right to know our hopes, our dreams, and our goals.

> We will get a great hotel for our guests, but what about us? We should have a great work environment, too. Besides the physical setting, the work environment is created by you—the work environment is the people who work here. We need to create a good work environment by respecting each other. But things go wrong. As soon as two people come together, conflict will arise. It's not the fact that we have conflict—it's what we do with it. Talk to your manager. It's not "them" or "they." We all have the same dream of excellence; we all have the same goal: to be successful.

Leadership Orientation

After spending time with all the employees together, Schulze conducted the Leadership Orientation for managers, and the tone changed:

> This business is created for one reason—to make money. This is your role. You have accepted the role, in the hotel business, to be businesspeople. No one in the world knows more about what our customers want than we do. We survey them every four weeks. What do these customers want? A clean hotel. I walk in hotels, see something on the floor, and I see you walking by it! It's incredible—inconceivable—for us to know what customers want and to

not do it. We still only deliver 92% of customers who are satisfied. That gives us occupancy of 80%. Why not celebrate? Only 8% are not satisfied.

Of those, 2% to 3% want things we cannot do, or things that, if we did them, would dissatisfy all of the other customers. But 5% represent satisfaction that we want. Those 5% are dissatisfied because of stupid, pathetic defects that are repeating—stupid, pathetic defects that you should have eliminated permanently. That 5% translates into 200,000 dissatisfied customers. That is an army—attacking us—saying that we are not good. If we satisfied this 5%, within three years we'd run at 88% occupancy. What does 88% mean in dollars? Three hundred million to the bottom line. We are leaving $300 million on the table because of 5% defects.

In addition to a strong commitment to the bottom line, Schulze saw leaders as having deep obligations to the rank-and-file employees:

Orientation is a key process to make sure you have the right employees. Why? Because an employee joins you open minded. Share with them what you dream about, what you wish for, your heart and soul, and then ask them to join you in your mission. They have a right to know who you are, what your dreams are.

People have a right to come to work for a purpose. The chairs that you are sitting on are doing work. If you don't give your employees a purpose, you make them chairs. If you just send them to work without a purpose, it's immoral.

Schulze's intense focus on purposeful work inspired many Ritz-Carlton employees to remain committed to the organization. For example, Vijay Singh explained his reasons for staying with the company: "I joined The Ritz-Carlton eight years ago because of a statement I heard made by Horst Schulze: 'I come to work for two reasons. One, to achieve excellence. The other, to achieve excellence with friends.' I adopted this philosophy in my own life and have stayed with The Ritz-Carlton because Mr. Schulze has not deviated from his vision."[7]

Day Two: Departmental Vision Sessions

On the second day of the Seven Day Countdown, employees in each functional area met for an introduction to their new departments. Group exercises were used to help the employees learn more about one another, their likes and dislikes, and how they could function together as an effective unit. Schulze kicked off the vision sessions for each department by asking the groups what they wanted to be in a year. The answer was invariably "the best," and Schulze started the process (later taken over by the managers) of specifying what being the best would mean for each area. In talking with the employees responsible for the bar and in-room service, Schulze explained:

In the case of the bar, customers are entering your room, but they are not coming for you. They are not coming to drink—they have drinks in their rooms and at home. They are not coming to eat. They are coming to *feel well*. You have to understand their purpose. The customer sets the pace; you capture the moments. You are in charge. Your charge is to help customers feel well. Your ultimate responsibility is that each guest feels well when they leave because of how you enhanced their life in the moment that you had to serve them.

---

[7] As quoted in *The Mystique: The Ritz-Carlton Hotel Company, L.L.C. Employee Newsletter*, Winter 2000.

In in-room service, you are entering their home, which they have rented. It requires a little different style, because it's their home, their private space. Ask them, "May I enter your room?" Part of being a lady and a gentleman is to treat the situation as a professional. They want you to leave as soon as possible. Ask them, "May I put the tray down here?" And be sure to thank them as you're leaving: "Thank you for allowing me to serve you." I want you to think about how you train yourself. There is only one way of teaching—self-teaching. Think, when you've left, where are you in creating a fine memory with your guest by how you behaved in the room?

Days Three through Seven: Skills Training

For the next five days, the hotel's leadership team, trainers, and managers met each morning at 6:00 a.m. to review the day's training activities and to resolve any difficulties that had arisen. Employees in the different functional areas were given a "Warm Welcome" by their managers at 8:30 each morning and a traditional Ritz-Carlton "Fond Farewell" every evening. During the first two of the remaining five days, uniform fittings were scheduled, personal grooming sessions were conducted, and employees were introduced to the daily lineup procedure.

All employees attended a session on the anticipation and handling of guest requests, conducted by McBride, while each department continued to formulate and refine its own philosophy and statement of goals. Overviews within functional areas oriented the new staff to the big picture within their divisions. Everyone received "life safety" instruction, was treated to a wine tasting, and enjoyed a product show which allowed each employee to learn more about the materials that would provide creature comforts to their guests.

"Instant guest pacification" was a Ritz-Carlton basic, and on Day Four all new employees were instructed in the standardized procedure for "Handling Guest Difficulties." Employees were trained to immediately break away from their normal activities to solve a customer's problem, to use their empowerment in designing an appropriate solution, and to involve and follow up with other departments whose help was needed. Each problem was documented on a Guest Incident Action form in which "guest temperature" was recorded before and after the event on a scale that ran from "livid" to "calm"; these forms were used for daily communication and process improvement (see **Exhibit 12**).

The last three days of the Seven Day Countdown was when departmental technical training occurred. Employees learned the details involved in performing their jobs to the standards set by The Ritz-Carlton, and everyone was expected to master their department's key production processes. Employees arrived in two shifts, dressed in their full uniforms, and every employee practiced his or her job as if they were serving real customers. For instance, mock meals were served, trials were conducted for check-in procedures, and housekeepers prepared rooms for "guests."

Members of the corporate steering committee observed every trial run, from housekeeping to restaurants. They were looking for any flaws in service delivery that kept it from being as sharp and crisp as The Ritz-Carlton demanded. Their observations were passed on to the trainers, who provided any necessary additional one-on-one or division-level training. Inghilleri recalled occasions when Schulze stepped in to assist a struggling employee: "He was just great. He'd go into a restaurant, and he'd say, 'OK, let me show you how this job is done,' and he'd give a perfect demonstration. When the president of your company is showing you how to do your job, you are really going to be paying attention."

Recognizing that their standards of service were extremely high and that their goal of opening as a top-notch hotel right from the start was a tall order, The Ritz-Carlton tried to protect their employees from feeling overwhelmed by controlling the occupancy rate. Inghilleri explained:

> The first month of operations, we may open the hotel with 50% occupancy. Then we'll increase occupancy monthly, so it takes us somewhere between three and four months to reach 80%. But we hire, in the very beginning, as if we're already operating at 80% occupancy.

> This allows us to reduce the number of tables a waiter has to serve, or the number of rooms a housekeeper has to clean. It is more important that we set the standards immediately. They have to do their jobs perfectly, even if it takes them longer; productivity will increase as they get more and more comfortable. Flawless execution is the goal, and then speed will come. This practice also allows us to offset the inevitable minor turnover that we experience shortly after opening.

On the day between the end of the Seven Day Countdown and the grand opening, employees showed up in casual attire for The Ritz-Carlton two-hour pep rally, marking the transition between practice runs and real service delivery. The next day, on October 11, 2000, the Washington, D.C., Ritz-Carlton Hotel opened for business.

Dilemma

McBride sat in his new office in Washington, reflecting on the concerns that Collins had expressed, with his usual blunt style and candor, about the Seven Day Countdown. Collins questioned whether the seven-day time frame limited the hotel's ability to open at a higher occupancy rate and to reach 80% occupancy in a shorter amount of time. Since the Seven Day Countdown was only a small part of the pre-opening budget (see **Exhibit 13**), the costs might well be worth the benefits. Because Collins wanted to ensure that the service established was flawless and a real draw for potential condominium residents, he questioned whether extra training would help the employees to further polish their service skills.

McBride acknowledged that the $700 million investment made by the Millennium Partners in six Ritz-Carlton-managed properties certainly gave Collins the right to voice his opinions. But it was one thing to change the kind of art in the hotels—changing the processes that seemed to finally join quality control and human resources in a perfect balance was something else entirely.

It was difficult to train new hires to meet the high expectations of The Ritz-Carlton service standards in only seven days, but that was how The Ritz-Carlton worked. True, sometimes the countdown occurred as the building itself was being completed. Sometimes, it seemed like they barely made it under the wire for opening day. Maybe the training should be longer, but what would that mean for The Ritz-Carlton? McBride would be responsible for opening the second Millennium Partners-owned Ritz-Carlton hotel, in Georgetown, at the end of 2001. Should he try changing the Seven Day Countdown process, which was a worldwide best practice for the company?

The Ritz-Carlton Hotel Company   601-163

Exhibit 1   Locations of Current and Future Ritz-Carlton and Four Seasons Properties

Asia/South Pacific		Europe/Middle East	
The Ritz-Carlton	**Four Seasons**	**The Ritz-Carlton**	**Four Seasons**
• **Bali**	• **Bali (2 resorts)**	• Berlin	• Berlin
• Hong Kong	• Hong Kong	• Istanbul (2001)	• Istanbul
• Kuala Lumpur	• Kuala Lumpur	• **Sharm El Sheikh, Egypt**	• Sharm El Sheikh (2001)
• Shanghai	• Shanghai (2001)		
• Singapore	• Singapore (2 hotels)	• Barcelona	• Alexandria, Egypt (2004)
		• **Doha, Qatar (2001)**	• Amman, Jordan (2002)
• Osaka	• Bangkok Chiang Mai at Mae Rim Valley	• Dubai, United Arab Emirates	• Beirut (2004)
• Seoul	• Jakarta	• Dusseldorf	• Budapest (2002)
	• Maldives at Kuda Huraa	• Wolfsburg, Germany	• Cairo (1 hotel existing; one planned for 2002)
	• Taipei		• Dublin (2001)
	• Tokyo		• Lisbon (The Ritz, managed by Four Seasons)
	• Sydney		• London
			• Milan
			• Paris
			• Prague (2001)
			• Riyadh, Saudi Arabia (2002)
The Americas and Caribbean			
The Ritz-Carlton	**Four Seasons**	**The Ritz-Carlton**	**Four Seasons**
• Atlanta (2 hotels)	• Atlanta	• **Laguna Niguel, CA (2002)**	• **Hualalai, HI**
• *Boston (1 hotel; Boston Common, 2001)*	• Boston	• Marina del Rey, CA	• Las Vegas, NV
• Houston (2002)	• Houston	• Montreal, Canada	• Los Angeles, CA (2 hotels)
• *New York (Central Park South, 2002; Downtown, 2001)*	• New York (2 hotels)	• **Naples, FL**	• Mexico, D.F.
		• **Naples Golf Resort (FL, 2001)**	• *Miami, FL (2002)*
• **Palm Beach, FL**	• **Palm Beach, FL**	• New Orleans, LA	• Newport Beach, CA
• Philadelphia	• Philadelphia	• Pasadena, CA	• **Papagayo Peninsula, Costa Rica (2002)**
• San Francisco	• *San Francisco (2001)*	• Pentagon City, VA	• **Punta Mita, Mexico**
• Toronto (2003)	• Toronto	• Phoenix, AZ	• **San Diego, CA**
• *Washington, D.C. (Foggy Bottom; Georgetown, 2002)*	• Washington, D.C.	• **Rancho Mirage, CA**	• **San Miguel, Mexico (2003)**
		• **Reynolds Plantation, GA (2002)**	• **Santa Barbara, CA**
• **Amelia Island, FL**	• Austin, TX	• **Rose Hall, Jamaica**	• **Scottsdale, AZ**
• **Cancun, Mexico**	• Caracas, Venezuela (2001)	• St. Louis, MO	• Seattle, WA
• Cleveland, OH	• Chicago, IL (one Four Seasons; The Ritz, managed by Four Seasons)	• **St. Thomas, Virgin Islands**	• Vancouver, Canada
• Coconut Grove, FL (2002)		• San Juan, Puerto Rico	• **Whistler, Canada (2003)**
• Dearborn, MI		• Sarasota, FL (2001)	
• **Grand Cayman**		• South Beach, FL (2001)	
• **Half Moon Bay, CA (2001)**	• **Dallas, TX**	• Tyson's Corner, VA	
• **Kapalua (Maui, HI)**	• **Grand Exuma, Bahamas (2002)**		
• **Key Biscayne, FL (2001)**			

Source: Ritz-Carlton locations were provided by The Ritz-Carlton Hotel Company, L.L.C. Four Seasons locations were obtained from www.fourseasons.com (accessed January 16, 2001). Locations in **bold** typeface are resorts; locations in *italicized* typeface are hotels and multi-use facilities owned by the Millennium Partners.

Exhibit 2   Key Operating Statistics for The Ritz-Carlton and Four Seasons[a]

	1999		1998		1997	
	The Ritz-Carlton	Four Seasons	The Ritz-Carlton	Four Seasons	The Ritz-Carlton	Four Seasons
Occupancy Rate	75.4%	70.0%	72.5%	70.4%	76.7%	73.7%
Average Daily Rate (ADR)	$202	$266	$194	$248	$187	$243
Revenue Per Available Room (RevPAR)	$152	$189	$140	$178	$145	$180

Sources: Ritz-Carlton data for 1999 and 1998 are from the 1999 and 1998 Marriott International Annual Reports. The Ritz-Carlton figures for 1997 were calculated based on reported changes in figures in the 1998 Marriott International Annual Report. The Four Seasons data was obtained from their 1999 Annual Report.

[a]All Four Seasons figures were converted from Canadian to U.S. dollars using the average exchange rate for the relevant year from International Monetary Fund data. Corporatewide figures were computed using weighted averages from the regionally reported information in the 1999 Four Seasons Annual Report.

Exhibit 3   The Ritz-Carlton Washington, D.C., 2001 First-Year Monthly Budget Summary[a]

	JAN	FEB	MAR	APR	MAY	JUN	JUL	AUG	SEP	OCT	NOV	DEC	YEAR
Revenue Drivers													
Room Nights Available	9,300	8,400	9,300	9,000	9,300	9,000	9,300	9,300	9,000	9,300	9,000	9,300	109,500
Room Nights Sold	5,318	5,145	6,645	6,381	7,083	6,689	4,817	4,628	6,661	7,624	6,340	4,193	71,524
% Occupancy	57.2%	61.3%	71.5%	70.9%	76.2%	74.3%	51.8%	49.8%	74.0%	82.0%	70.4%	45.1%	65.3%
Average Daily Rate (ADR)	$305.32	$299.36	$312.08	$305.71	$305.44	$291.97	$263.08	$246.48	$322.76	$345.38	$302.88	$289.85	$302.44
Revenue Per Available Room (RevPAR)	$174.64	$183.51	$223.14	$216.75	$232.75	$216.93	$136.48	$122.75	$238.84	$283.21	$213.23	$130.72	$197.49
Sales and Income													
Rooms	1,624	1,540	2,074	1,951	2,163	1,953	1,267	1,141	2,150	2,633	1,920	1,215	21,631
Food and Beverage	1,314	1,195	1,686	1,721	1,957	1,907	1,146	1,047	1,747	1,949	1,510	1,617	18,796
Telephone	69	67	86	83	91	86	63	60	86	98	82	54	925
Retail	12	11	15	14	16	15	11	10	15	17	16	27	179
Recreation/Spa	4	4	5	5	5	5	4	4	5	6	5	3	54
Garage	111	107	138	132	147	138	100	96	138	157	131	87	1,482
Other Income	51	49	61	59	65	61	47	45	61	69	59	42	668
Total Revenue	3,184	2,973	4,064	3,965	4,444	4,166	2,637	2,403	4,202	4,929	3,724	3,046	43,736
Allocated Expenses													
Rooms	500	479	560	545	580	559	464	456	555	607	538	448	6,291
Food and Beverage	1,049	1,011	1,315	1,339	1,478	1,460	977	917	1,354	1,484	1,210	1,303	14,898
Telephone	42	39	44	43	45	43	41	41	43	46	42	39	506
Retail	12	11	13	13	13	13	11	11	13	14	14	19	157
Recreation/Spa	3	3	4	3	4	4	3	2	4	4	3	2	38
Garage	105	98	117	113	121	116	101	99	116	126	113	94	1,321
Other Income	25	25	30	29	31	30	24	23	30	33	29	21	329
Total Allocated Expenses	1,736	1,665	2,083	2,085	2,273	2,224	1,620	1,549	2,114	2,314	1,950	1,927	23,540
Unallocated Expenses													
Administration and General	247	229	267	252	266	249	226	223	262	277	250	245	2,994
Marketing and Sales	222	193	229	224	233	220	199	198	231	244	222	213	2,628
Heat, Light, and Power	53	52	57	51	54	52	41	39	50	57	54	46	607
Repairs and Maintenance	135	127	135	131	134	131	130	130	131	135	130	134	1,583
Total Unallocated Expenses	657	600	688	658	687	652	507	591	674	713	657	637	7,812

[a] All figures are disguised. All monetary figures except ADR and RevPAR are in $1,000s.

Exhibit 3 (continued)

	JAN	FEB	MAR	APR	MAY	JUN	JUL	AUG	SEP	OCT	NOV	DEC	YEAR
House Profit	791	708	1,293	1,222	1,484	1,289	420	264	1,414	1,901	1,117	481	12,384
Other Deductions													
Management Fee Base	104	97	133	129	145	136	86	78	137	162	122	98	1,429
Management Fee Incentive	0	0	0	0	0	0	0	0	0	0	0	0	0
Capital Expenditure													
Program Reserve	31	29	39	38	43	40	25	23	40	95	72	58	532
Property Taxes	117	117	117	117	117	117	117	117	117	117	117	117	1,400
Insurance	15	15	15	15	15	15	15	15	15	15	15	15	175
Leases and Other	5	5	5	5	5	5	5	5	5	5	5	5	60
Ground Rent	0	0	0	0	0	0	0	0	0	0	0	0	0
Total Other Deductions	271	262	308	304	324	312	248	238	314	393	330	292	3,596
Cash Before Debt	520	445	984	919	1,160	978	173	26	1,100	1,508	787	189	8,788
Debt Service	0	0	0	0	0	0	0	0	0	0	0	0	0
Cash After Debt	520	445	984	919	1,160	978	173	26	1,100	1,508	787	189	8,788

Source: The Ritz-Carlton Hotel Company, L.L.C.

The Ritz-Carlton Hotel Company   601-163

Exhibit 4   Partial Organizational Charts for The Ritz-Carlton and Millennium Partners in 2000

The Ritz-Carlton

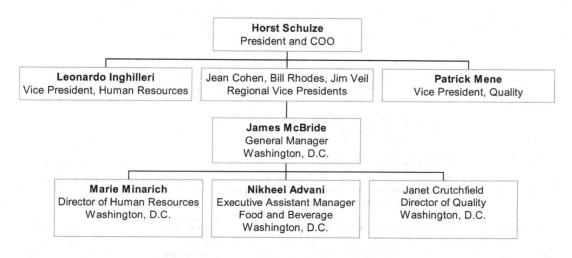

Millennium Partners

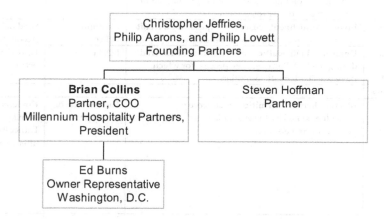

Source: The Ritz-Carlton and Millennium Partners.

601-163

Exhibit 5 Service Quality Indicators (SQIs)

Key Production Process	Service Quality Indicators	Measurement Location	Reporting Requirements
Individual and Group Reservations	**Abandoned Calls**: those that are not answered and the customer hangs up	Reservation Office	Send daily to Department of Quality (DOQ) by close of Reservation Office
Anticipation of Guest Needs	**Missing Preferences**: regular guest arrivals (i.e., five or more visits to your city hotel, three or more visits to your resort hotel) whose profile lacks actionable preferences beyond room type, smoking preference, or title	Guest Recognition Office	Send daily by 5:00 p.m. to DOQ
Warm Welcome/ Check-In	**Unready Guest Rooms**: any guest room that is not immediately ready for the guest when they arrive to register, regardless of the time of day; includes room re-locations during guest Check-In	At point of Check-In	Send daily by end of second shift to DOQ
Guest Room Assignment	**Room Changes**: guest requests a change of room after Check-In	Front Office	Send daily by end of second shift to DOQ
Guest Room Condition	**Room Condition**: customer requests repairs to their guest room	All Departments	Send daily by end of second shift to DOQ
Housekeeping	**Housekeeping Defects**: total score of housekeeping defects identified during five random daily inspections	Guest Rooms	Send daily by 5:00 p.m. to DOQ
Hotel Cleanliness	**Unacceptable Appearance of Public Area**: identified during the Morning Process	Public Areas	Send immediately after daily inspections to DOQ
Problem Resolution	**Missing or Damaged Guest Property/Accident**: number of claims/incidents for the disappearance or damage of guest property (i.e., vehicles, vehicle keys, luggage, clothing, jewelry, valuables, etc.) or accidents involving a guest or employee that require care from a medical professional	At the time the incident is reported	Send to DOQ immediately after each incident
Problem Resolution	**Invoice Adjustment**: customer requests for a credit or refund for real or perceived deficiencies	Accounting Office	Send daily by close of the Accounting Office to DOQ
Problem Resolution	**Unresolved Difficulties**: any difficulty discovered during the J. D. Power survey process for which there was inadequate resolution	J.D. Power	Fax to DOQ after each occurrence
Meeting Events:			
1. Desire for Business 2. Communication of the Program 3. Flexibility in Negotiations 4. Advise of Conflicts 5. Audio-Visual	**Meeting Event Difficulties**: total score of difficulties stated by the event planner during the post-event conversation	Face-to-face, or by telephone	Conference Services Manager submits Event Difficulty Log to DOQ after each conversation
Food & Beverage:			
1. Restaurants, Lounge, & Club	**Composite Score**: checks opened or adjusted because of customer dissatisfaction of any type	Within the Outlet	Send daily as soon as possible to DOQ
2. Room Service	**Room Service Orders**: those orders delivered past the company standard commitment time or delivery of incomplete orders	Room Service	Send daily at the end of each shift to DOQ
3. Banquet Food	**Banquet Event Difficulties**	Banquet Floor	Banquet Office submits report after each event

Source: The Ritz-Carlton Hotel Company, L.L.C.

The Ritz-Carlton Hotel Company   601-163

Exhibit 6   Awards Won by The Ritz-Carlton

The Malcolm Baldrige National Quality Award
- 1992: First and only hotel company to win the award
- 1999: First and only service company to win the award two times

AAA Five Diamond Awards
- 10 properties and 6 restaurants (2001)
- 11 properties (2000)
- The first ever AAA Triple Five Diamond Hotel (1999)

Conde Nast Traveler, Business Travel Awards
- Best European Hotel Chain for Business Travel (2000)
- #3 North American Hotel Chain for Business Travel (2000)
- #5 Asia/Pacific Hotel Chain for Business Travel (2000)
- Best Hotel Chain in Asia-Pacific (1998)
- Best Club Floors in the World (1998)

Conde Nast Traveler, 2000 Gold List
- 16 properties on The Gold List
- "The only urban hotel with two perfect scores for service and rooms"
- "The highest-scoring property in the Americas"
- "The highest-scoring property for service in the United States"

Conde Nast Traveler, 1999 Readers' Choice Awards
- #2 "Best of the Best"
- #1 Asian Hotel
- #1 and #2 North American Resorts
- #3 North American Hotel
- #1 Australian Hotel
- #1 Caribbean/Latin Hotel
- #1 Caribbean/Atlantic Resort

East Magazine
- Three of Asia's Best Business Hotels (2000)

Far Eastern Economic Review
- Named one of Asia's 200 Leading Companies (1999)

Florida Living Magazine, 2000 Best of Florida Award
- "Best Resort"

Globo Magazine
- Best Hotel Company in the World (1999)

Gourmet Magazine
- Best Hotel in Mexico (1999)
- Tops for Romance (1999)
- #6 Hotel in the World, Rooms at the Top Survey (1999)
- Best Hotel Chain or Group – United States and the World (1998)

Mobil Travel Guide Five Star Awards
- The Ritz-Carlton, Naples (2000, 2001)
- The Dining Room at The Ritz-Carlton, Buckhead (2000)

Official Hotel Guide
- Gold Award for "Favorite Deluxe Hotel Chain, North America" (1998)

Senses, Wellness Award 2000
- "Best Beach Resort"
- #2, "Your Personal Favorite as Overall Winner"

Travel & Leisure, 2001 Best Value Hotels
- The Ritz-Carlton, Bali
- The Ritz-Carlton, Montreal

Travel & Leisure, World's Best Awards (1999)
- Six of the Top 100 Hotels in the World
- #1 Hotel in: the Continental U.S. & Canada; Hawaii; Mexico, Central, & South America; The Caribbean, Bermuda, & Bahamas; and Australia, New Zealand, & the South Pacific

Travel & Leisure, World's Best Service Awards (1999)
- Five properties with World's Best Service
- #1 in service in: Hawaii; Mexico, Central, & South America; and Australia, New Zealand, & the South Pacific

Worth Magazine, Readers' Choice Award
- Best Luxury Hotel Chain (2000)

Zagat U.S. Hotels, Resorts, & Spas Survey
- Best Hotel Chain (1990, 1993, 1995)

Source: The Ritz-Carlton Hotel Company, L.L.C.

Exhibit 7   The Ritz-Carlton Post-Opening Training and Development Program

	Phase 1		
	Line Staff	Middle Manager	General Manager
• Hotel Orientation (16 hours; *for new hotels, part of 7-Day Countdown*)	X		
• Training Certification (120 hours; *begins during 7-Day Countdown*)	X		
• Day 21 (4 hours)	X	X	X
• Leadership Orientation (4 days, 32 hours)		X	X
• If possible, participate in new hotel opening (2 weeks, 100 hours)		X	X
• 2 days in corporate office meeting with senior leaders (16 hours)			X
• 2 weeks in a functioning hotel in the same class or level (100 hours)			X
	Phase 2		
	Line Staff	Middle Manager	General Manager
• Hotel Orientation (2 days/16 hours)	X	X	X
• GLOW (Guest Problem Resolution process; 3 hours)	X	Within 5 months of entering Phase 2	Within 5 months of entering Phase 2
• LEAP (Advanced Guest Problem Resolution and up-selling skills; 4 hours)	X	Within 5 months of entering Phase 2	Within 5 months of entering Phase 2
• Understanding How a Talent-Based Organization works (attend if a Departmental Trainer; 8 hours)	X	Within 5 months of entering Phase 2	Within 5 months of entering Phase 2
• Creating an environment of trust and empowerment (5 hours)	X	Within 5 months of entering Phase 2	Within 5 months of entering Phase 2
• CARE (Controlling Alcohol Risks Effectively; 3 hours)	X	Within 5 months of entering Phase 2	Within 5 months of entering Phase 2
• Food Safety (2 hours)	X	Within 5 months of entering Phase 2	Within 5 months of entering Phase 2
• Day 365 (3 hours)	X	Within 5 months of entering Phase 2	Within 5 months of entering Phase 2
• Re-certification (10 hours)	X	For departments in division; Within 5 months of entering Phase 2	
• Re-orientation (4 hours)	X	Within 5 months of entering Phase 2	Within 5 months of entering Phase 2
• TARGET (train the trainer on Ritz-Carlton training certification process, 5 hours)		Within 5 months of entering Phase 2	Within 5 months of entering Phase 2
• Situational Leadership (16 hours)		Within 5 months of entering Phase 2	Within 5 months of entering Phase 2
• The Seven Habits of Highly Effective People (32 hours)		Within 5 months of entering Phase 2	Within 5 months of entering Phase 2
• Understanding training certification in each role in department and division		Ongoing for first 3 weeks of Phase 2	
	Phase 3		
	Line Staff	Middle Manager	General Manager
• Leadership Center for advanced management skills (2 days/16 hours)		X	X
TOTAL TRAINING HOURS	**174**	**279**	**349**

Source: The Ritz-Carlton Hotel Company, L.L.C.

Exhibit 8   Product Quality Indicators (PQIs)

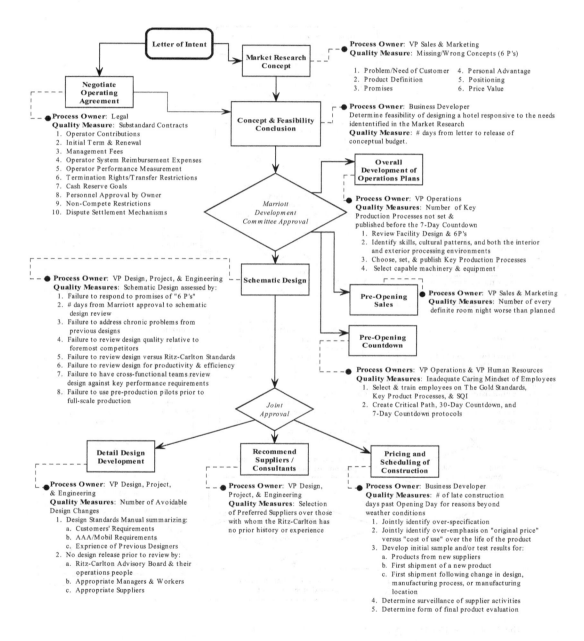

Source: The Ritz-Carlton Hotel Company, L.L.C.

Exhibit 9 Pre-Employment Call-Back Process

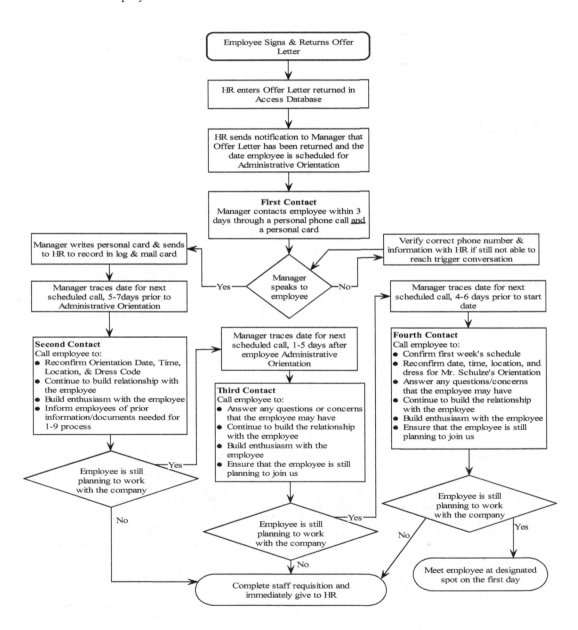

Source: The Ritz-Carlton Hotel Company, L.L.C

Exhibit 10   The "Paper Palm"

Warm Welcome

[handwritten note]

Welcome to the team that is going to recreate Service Excellence.

The next few weeks will be challenging, but the rewards will be great.

I thank you for your commitment and hard work.

Warm regards,

[signature]

The Ritz-Carlton, Washington, D.C. Paper Palm   4

Mission Statement

The Ritz-Carlton, Washington, D.C.

The Ritz-Carlton will redefine the service business in Washington, D.C. by building a world class reputation as a result of the loyalty created through our commitment to our guests, employees and owners.

By providing innovative, five-star, five-diamond service enhanced by cutting edge technology, The Ritz-Carlton will be the first choice for guests in Washington, D.C.

As the leader, we will fulfill our obligation to our Owners and The Ritz-Carlton Hotel Company, L.L.C. to achieve Product and Profit Dominance.

The Ritz-Carlton, Washington, D.C. Paper Palm   5

- Positions and names of the Corporate Steering Committee and the Hotel Guidance Team
- Background regarding Marriott International and Millennium Partners
- Descriptions of the artwork in the hotel and information about the various artists
- General schedule of the Seven Day Countdown

Additional Information Contained in the "Paper Palm"

- Descriptions of guest rooms and rates
- Hours of operation for restaurants, communications center, sports club, & gift shop
- Diagram of meeting facilities
- Descriptions of the Sports Club/LA and the Splash Spa

- Spaces to write down key extensions for services such as the concierge, housekeeping, guest services, restaurant reservations, and room service
- Appropriate verbiage for employees to use when communicating with guests, such as: "Good afternoon," "Have a pleasant day," "How may I assist you?," "I beg your pardon," "Please forgive me," "Excellent choice," "My pleasure."

27

Source: The Ritz-Carlton Hotel Company, L.L.C.

601-163   The Ritz-Carlton Hotel Company

Exhibit 11   The Gold Standards

THREE STEPS OF SERVICE	THE MOTTO	THE EMPLOYEE PROMISE	THE CREDO
1 A warm and sincere greeting. Use the guest name, if and when possible. 2 Anticipation and compliance with guest needs. 3 Fond Farewell. Give them a warm good-bye and use their names, if and when possible.	*We Are Ladies and Gentlemen Serving Ladies and Gentlemen*	*At The Ritz-Carlton, our Ladies and Gentlemen are the most important resource in our service commitment to our guests.* *By applying the principles of trust, honesty, respect, integrity, and commitment, we nurture and maximize talent to the benefit of each individual and the company.* *The Ritz-Carlton fosters a work environment where diversity is valued, quality of life enhanced, individual aspirations are fulfilled, and The Ritz-Carlton mystique is strengthened.*	The Ritz-Carlton Hotel is a place where the genuine care and comfort of our guests is our highest mission. We pledge to provide the finest personal service and facilities for our guests who will always enjoy a warm, relaxed, yet refined ambiance. The Ritz-Carlton experience enlivens the senses, instills well-being, and fulfills even the unexpressed wishes and needs of our guests.

The Ritz-Carlton Basics

1. The Credo is the principal belief of our Company. It must be known, owned, and energized by all.
2. Our Motto is: "We are Ladies and Gentlemen Serving Ladies and Gentlemen." As service professionals, we treat our guests and each other with respect and dignity.
3. The Three Steps of Service are the foundation of Ritz-Carlton hospitality. These steps must be used in every interaction to ensure satisfaction, retention, and loyalty.
4. The Employee Promise is the basis for our Ritz-Carlton work environment. It will be honored by all employees.
5. All employees will successfully complete annual training certification for their position.
6. Company Objectives are communicated to all employees. It is everyone's responsibility to support them.
7. To create pride and joy in the workplace, all employees have the right to be involved in the planning of the work that affects them.
8. Each employee will continuously identify defects (M.R. B.I.V.) throughout the Hotel.
9. It is the responsibility of each employee to create a work environment of teamwork and lateral service so that the needs of our guests and each other are met.
10. Each employee is empowered. For example, when a guest has a problem or needs something special, you should break away from your regular duties to address and resolve the issue.
11. Uncompromising levels of cleanliness are the responsibility of every employee.
12. To provide the finest personal service for our guests, each employee is responsible for identifying and recording individual guest preferences.
13. Never lose a guest. Instant guest pacification is the responsibility of each employee. Whoever receives a complaint will own it, resolve it to the guest's satisfaction, and record it.
14. "Smile – We are on stage." Always maintain positive eye contact. Use the proper vocabulary with our guests and each other. (Use words like "Good Morning," "Certainly," "I'll be happy to," and "My pleasure").
15. Be an ambassador of your Hotel in and outside of the workplace. Always speak positively. Communicate any concerns to the appropriate person.
16. Escort guests rather than pointing out directions to another area of the Hotel.
17. Use Ritz-Carlton telephone etiquette. Answer within three rings with a "smile." Use the guest's name when possible. When necessary, ask the caller "May I place you on hold?" Do not screen calls. Eliminate call transfers whenever possible. Adhere to voice mail standards.
18. Take pride in and care of your personal appearance. Everyone is responsible for conveying a professional image by adhering to Ritz-Carlton clothing and grooming standards.
19. Think safety first. Each employee is responsible for creating a safe, secure, and accident-free environment for all guests and each other. Be aware of all fire and safety emergency procedures, and report any security risks immediately.
20. Protecting the assets of a Ritz-Carlton Hotel is the responsibility of every employee. Conserve energy, properly maintain our Hotels, and protect the environment.

Source: The Ritz-Carlton Hotel Company, L.L.C.

The Ritz-Carlton Hotel Company   601-163

Exhibit 12   Handling Guest Difficulties

Handling Guest Difficulties Procedure

1. **Break away from work**. Basic #10 (Call someone if you can't break away.)

2. **Instant Guest Pacification.** Basic #13

3. **LEAP**.

    a. Listen

    b. Empathize

    c. **A**sk for Clarification. Take notes if necessary.

    d. **P**roduce a Solution. Use your empowerment. If you cannot do it yourself, ask your Manager for help. Follow up with other departments involved in solution.

4. **Complete QIA.** (Distribute to all departments if applicable).

5. **Follow-up within 20 minutes**. To find out if the guest is satisfied with the solution.

THE RITZ-CARLTON, WASHINGTON, D.C.
QIA: Guest Incident Action Form

Incident Date: Time:

Guest Name:			Company Affiliation (if applicable):		
Address:			Telephone Number:		
Room Number:		Arrival Date:		Departure Date:	
GUEST TEMPERATURE					
Before:	Livid	Very Upset	Upset	OK	Calm
After:	Livid	Very Upset	Upset	OK	Calm
What Was *The Problem*?					
What Did You Do *To Resolve The Problem*?					
Was The Opportunity *Resolved to the Guest Satisfaction*? Yes NO					
Recommended Follow Up Action Steps:					
Employees Involved:			Form Completed By: Department: Date Completed:		

Please note: this is a legal document. Include *facts* only.

E-Mail to GRP RC Washington DC Everyone or Place A Copy in the Mailboxes

HANDLING GUEST DIFFICULTIES: PROCESS MANAGEMENT

WHAT	WHO, WHEN
1. Print and include in line-up packet for next day distribution: • QIAs • Summary of in-house guests with difficulties	Night Manager, daily overnight
2. Print and include in line-up packet for next day distribution: • "Outstanding Difficulties Report"	Night Manager, overnight on Fridays
3. Ensure QIA's are followed up personally with guest and QIA originator.	GT & Dept. Heads. Daily
4. Analysis of top difficulties by hotel and departments • Action Plans for the 20 of the 80 should be designed	Department of Quality: Quarterly

Source: The Ritz-Carlton Hotel Company L.L.C.

601-163   The Ritz-Carlton Hotel Company

Exhibit 13   The Ritz-Carlton Washington, D.C., Pre-Opening Budget

SALARIES & WAGES		OTHER EXPENSES	
Food & Beverage Division		*Sales and Marketing*	
Banquets	49,990	Association Dues	4,003
Catering	136,383	Brochures & Direct Mail	106,780
F & B Executive	43,264	Entertainment	50,000
Honor Bar	3,505	Miscellaneous	25,000
Kitchen	101,517	Operating Supplies & Production	65,000
Lobby Lounge	9,767	Print Media	151,085
Restaurant Reservations	2,998	Public Relations	45,000
Room Service	11,135	Site Visit Expense	29,000
Stewarding	21,483	Telephone	40,000
Storeroom	3,960	Trade Shows	25,000
The Bar	5,950	Travel	60,000
The Restaurant	24,892	VIP Guest Gifts	10,000
Total Food & Beverage Division	**414,844**	**Total Sales and Marketing**	**610,868**
Rooms Division		*Operational and Office Expenses*	
Business Center	7,108	Duplicating/Fax	10,000
Concierge	9,170	Hotel Forms	40,000
Front Office	30,096	Menus and Check Presenters	55,000
Housekeeping	74,621	Office Rental/Equipment	39,500
Telephone	17,810	Office Supplies	20,000
Reservations	39,092	Postage	10,000
Rooms Executive	38,630	Telephone	35,004
Service Staff	9,650	**Total Operational Office Expenses**	**209,504**
The Club	7,970		
Total Rooms Division	**234,147**	*Selection, Orientation & Training*	
		Advertising	5,000
Other Departments		Mass Selection	5,000
Accounting	176,343	Travel (Interviews)	10,000
Cafeteria	28,569	Talent Plus Executive Interview	5,000
Engineering	115,680	Presentation Costs[a]	5,000
Executive	137,128	Trainers[a]	40,000
Human Resources	80,762	Pep Rally[a]	5,000
Laundry	40,298	**Total Orientation & Training**	**75,000**
Purchasing	39,030		
Sales & Marketing	409,642	*Recipe Testing/Trial Feedings*	
Security	20,174	Banquets	4,000
Sundry Shop	5,065	Chef's Table[a]	2,500
Total Other Departments	**1,052,691**	Employee Cafeteria[b]	30,000
Other Compensation		Food Shows[a]	7,000
Incentive Compensation	161,527	Kitchen Prep	28,000
Payroll Taxes & Employee Benefits	357,340	Lobby Lounge	2,500
Relocation	165,077	Non-perishables	40,000
Total Other Compensation	**683,944**	Room Service	2,000
		The Bar	3,000
Total Salaries & Wages	**2,385,626**	The Restaurant	20,000
		Total Recipe Testing/Trial Feedings	**139,000**
Miscellaneous			
Entertainment	10,000	**TOTAL EXPENSES**	**3,500,000**
Executive Committee Travel	25,000		
Miscellaneous	24,000		
Travel	21,002		
Total Miscellaneous	**80,002**		

NOTES:
[a] *Part of the Seven Day Countdown*
[b] *Half of the Employee Cafeteria Costs are part of the Seven Day Countdown*

Source: The Ritz-Carlton Hotel Company, L.L.C. **All figures are disguised.**

H A R V A R D | B U S I N E S S | S C H O O L

9-504-094
REV: SEPTEMBER 14, 2004

YOUNGME MOON

IKEA Invades America

In 2002, the IKEA Group was the world's top furniture retailer. With sales approaching $12 billion, IKEA operated 154 stores in 22 countries and serviced 286 million customers a year. (See **Exhibits 1** through **4**.) In the United States, IKEA had 14 stores, with plans to open as many as nine more in 2003. There were a number of factors that distinguished IKEA from other furniture retailers—its stores were strictly self-service and featured such amenities as playrooms for children and Swedish cafés, and all of its furniture came unassembled (customers were expected to put together the furniture on their own)—yet there was no question about the company's success; when a new store opened, it was not unusual for thousands of shoppers to line up on the first day.

Company Background

IKEA was founded in 1943 when 17-year-old Ingvar Kamprad decided to start a local catalog company using some money his father had given him.[1] Initially, the company sold basic household goods at discount prices; in 1947, however, Kamprad began selling home furnishings. Six years later, Kamprad opened his first furniture showroom, and two years after that, IKEA began designing its own low-priced furniture. In 1958, IKEA opened its inaugural store, in Almhult, Sweden; at 6,700 square meters, it was the largest furniture display in Scandinavia at the time.

By the time IKEA opened its flagship store in Stockholm in 1965, IKEA had become the favored furniture-shopping destination for price-conscious Swedes. The 45,800-square-meter flagship—which ultimately became the prototype for all of IKEA's retail outlets—was inspired by New York's Guggenheim Museum and featured a childcare center, a restaurant, a bank, and enough parking for 1,000 cars. The store's magnetic appeal was apparent from the start; literally thousands of Swedes showed up on the first day. Before long, IKEA was opening similar low-priced furniture stores in countries beyond Scandinavia, first in Europe, and then in both Asia and North America. (For a more detailed history, see **Figure A** below.)

---

[1] The name IKEA came from Kamprad's initials combined with the first letters of the names of the family farm (Elmtaryd) and village (Agunnaryd) where Kamprad was raised.

Professor Youngme Moon prepared this case. This case was developed from published sources. HBS cases are developed solely as the basis for class discussion. Cases are not intended to serve as endorsements, sources of primary data, or illustrations of effective or ineffective management.

Figure A   Significant Events in IKEA's Early History (excerpted from the IKEA Web site)

Date	Event
1926	**The founder of IKEA, Ingvar Kamprad, is born**. He was raised on a farm called Elmtaryd, near the small village of Agunnaryd. Even as a young boy, Ingvar knew that he wanted to develop a business. He started by selling matches to neighbors from his bicycle. He found that he could buy matches in bulk very cheaply from Stockholm and sell them individually at a very low price but still make a good profit.
1943	**IKEA is founded by Kamprad**. In 1943, when Ingvar was 17, his father gave him a gift for succeeding in his studies. The gift was used to establish his own business.
1947	**Furniture is introduced into the IKEA product range**. The furniture was produced by local manufacturers in the forests close to Kamprad's home.
1951	**The first IKEA furniture catalog is published**. Kamprad soon made the decision to discontinue all of the other products and focus directly on low-priced furniture, and the IKEA we know today was born.
1953	**The furniture showroom is opened in Almhult**. For the first time customers could see and touch our furnishings before ordering.
1955	**IKEA begins designing its own furniture**. There were several reasons for IKEA to start designing its own furniture. But what actually led to this—possibly our best move ever—was quite ironic. Pressure from our competitors caused suppliers to boycott IKEA. This reaction to our early success required us to begin designing our own furniture, and became the basis for future growth. Ultimately, this would lead to innovative design and improved function at lower prices. Then, by lucky inspiration, one early IKEA employee decided to remove a table's legs so it would fit into a car, and to avoid transport damage. From that point on, we began to think in terms of design for flat packaging. Which led to even further price reductions for our customers.
1956	**IKEA begins testing flat packages**. Designing products so that they can be packed flat and assembled by our customers greatly reduced their cost. This was obvious from the very first day we took the legs off a table and put it in a car. We can ship more items in one truck, less storage space is required, labor costs are reduced and transport damages are avoided. For the customer, this means lower priced products and easy transportation home.
1958	**The first IKEA store is inaugurated in Almhult**. 6,700 square meters of home furnishings! At the time, it was the largest furniture display in Scandinavia.
1965	**The IKEA store in Stockholm is opened**. Thousands of people waited for the opening of our flagship store. The 45,800 square meter store has a circular design, inspired by New York's Guggenheim Museum. The success created huge capacity problems in serving the customers. By opening the warehouse and letting people serve themselves, an important part of the IKEA concept was born.

Source: Used with the permission of Inter IKEA Systems B. V.

By 2002, IKEA was the world's most prominent furniture retailer. Although the company was privately held and did not release profit figures, its 2002 revenues approached $12 billion (see **Exhibit 1**) and its brand was considered to be one of the most valuable in the world.[2] Yet despite its success, IKEA's corporate culture still retained its pragmatic, cost-cutting sensibility. Waste was considered a deadly sin at IKEA; employees were constantly reminded to save on electricity by turning off lights and computers that were not in use, and managers always traveled coach and took buses instead of taxis if possible. In addition, all of the company's 70,000 employees were on a first-name basis, regardless of seniority or position. As one American who worked in IKEA's Almhult offices put it, "It's a little religious or missionary in a sense, but it's who we are."[3]

IKEA's Product Strategy

At IKEA, the new-product development process was overseen by a product-strategy council, which consisted of a group of senior managers who established priorities for IKEA's product lineup. These priorities were based on consumer trends, as identified by the globe-trotting council members. Once a product priority was established, a product developer would set the product's target retail price using what the company referred to as "the matrix." The matrix consisted of three basic price ranges and four basic styles (see **Figure B** below). Within each price range, the company would survey the competition to establish a benchmark and then set its own price point 30% to 50% lower than those of its rivals.

Figure B   IKEA's Product/Price Matrix

		STYLE			
		Scandinavian (sleek wood)	Modern (minimalist)	Country (neo-traditional)	Young Swede (bare bones)
PRICE RANGE	high				
	medium				
	low				

Source: Case author.

There was a separate matrix for each product type IKEA sold—that is, a price matrix for sofas, a price matrix for kitchen tables, and so on. In addition to being used to set retail prices, the matrix was used to identify gaps in the company's product lineup. By plotting the company's current product offerings on the grid and looking for empty spaces, product managers could readily identify market opportunities.

---

[2] In 2002, InterBrand, a marketing research firm, ranked IKEA 44th on its list of the world's most valuable brands, ahead of Apple, Pepsi, MTV, Harley-Davidson, and Xerox. See "The 100 Best Global Brands by Value," <www.interbrand.com>.

[3] Quote from Lisa Margonelli, "How IKEA Designs Its Sexy Price Tags," *Business 2.0*, October 2002.

Once IKEA had established the target retail price for the proposed product, the company would then begin selecting a manufacturer to produce it. IKEA worked with 1,800 suppliers in more than 50 countries, always seeking to balance cost-efficient labor with the company's product quality standards. (To save money on labor and production, the company was constantly on the lookout for opportunities to build supplier relationships in developing countries. See **Exhibits 5** and **6** for details.) IKEA would circulate a description of the proposed product's specifications and target cost to its suppliers and encourage them to compete for the production package.[4] In some cases, different product components would be sourced from different suppliers; for example, a supplier in Poland might produce a chair's cushion while a Chinese supplier might produce its frame. The two pieces would only come together in the store, when a consumer would select each piece individually.

Meanwhile, IKEA's engineers would determine what materials would be used to make the product. Here too, the focus was always on cost efficiency: the company liked to use high-quality materials (e.g., expensive wood) on furniture surfaces that were visible and most likely to undergo stress, and lower-quality materials (e.g., lower-grade wood or particleboard) on surfaces that were low stress and less visible to the consumer (e.g., inside the drawers). It was not uncommon for a single wooden product to contain as many as five different parts of the tree.

Once a price point was established, a manufacturer was in place, and the materials decided upon, the actual design process would begin. Although design was handled in-house, IKEA would once again use internal competition to select a designer. The company would circulate a product brief to its designers; this brief would include the product's price, its function, the materials to be used, and the manufacturer's capabilities. (IKEA had a pool of about 10 staff designers, but it also used many freelancers.) After designers submitted their design proposals, the company would select the best one.

Because the company's furniture was designed to ship disassembled, all of its products were transported "flat"; that is, in flat-packaged boxes. This flat packaging not only made it easier for consumers to transport the furniture home, it also saved the company on shipping (one of the company's mantras was, "We don't want to pay to ship air"[5]). In fact, the company estimated that its transport volume was six times less than if it shipped its products assembled.

Even after a new product ended up in IKEA's stores, the design process was not necessarily finished. It was not unusual for IKEA to redesign a product multiple times, with a single purpose in mind: To maximize the number of products that could be squeezed onto a shipping pallet. Of course, these redesigns would often increase the product assembly burden on the consumer. However, the constant focus on shipping frugality also meant that, with each new redesign, a product's retail price could remain stable over time (or even go down) while its shipping costs went down.

Low Price with Meaning

In IKEA's early days, the company's focus was primarily on price. Because of this, while IKEA enjoyed much early success, its low-priced furniture was functional at best, ugly at worst. As one design expert put it, "If you look at the history of IKEA, in the early years their design was quite horrible." In the last decade, however, this had changed as the company had gradually but

---

[4] IKEA owned some of its suppliers, but even these company-owned suppliers had to compete against independent contractors for IKEA's business.

[5] Quote from Lisa Margonelli, "How IKEA Designs Its Sexy Price Tags," *Business 2.0*, October 2002.

deliberately adopted a more distinct design aesthetic. "They became more and more interested in design," the expert noted. "Today if you go to IKEA, you always will find some pieces which are good designs and very reasonable in pricing."[6]

The company's corporate slogan—"Low price with meaning"—captured this commitment to offering tasteful, cleverly designed products that did not make customers feel cheap. Even the most basic products were now fashioned to reflect the company's philosophy of "democratic design." (See **Figure C** below for IKEA's vision statement.) And while no one in the company would claim that IKEA furniture was built for longevity—indeed, customers often discovered that IKEA products fell apart after a few years and had trouble withstanding anything as disruptive as a move to a new apartment—most of IKEA's customers were nonetheless delighted by their unique combination of form, function, and affordability.

Figure C   IKEA's Vision Statement: "Democratic Design: Low Price with Meaning"

A better everyday life.

The IKEA business idea is to offer a wide range of home furnishings with good design and function at prices so low that as many people as possible will be able to afford them. And still have money left!

Most of the time, beautifully designed home furnishings are created for a small part of the population—the few who can afford them. From the beginning, IKEA has taken a different path. We have decided to side with the many.

That means responding to the home furnishings needs of people throughout the world. People with many different needs, tastes, dreams, aspirations… and wallets. People who want to improve their homes and create better everyday lives.

It's not difficult to manufacture expensive fine furniture. Just spend the money and let the customers pay. To manufacture beautiful, durable furniture at low prices is not so easy. It requires a different approach. Finding simple solutions, scrimping and saving in every direction. Except on ideas.

But we can't do it alone. Our business idea is based on a partnership with the customer. First we do our part. Our designers work with manufacturers to find smart ways to make furniture using existing production processes. Then our buyers look all over the world for good suppliers with the most suitable raw materials. Next, we buy in bulk—on a global scale—so that we can get the best deals, and you can get the lowest prices.

Then you do your part. Using the IKEA catalog and visiting the store, you choose the furniture yourself and pick it up at the self-service warehouse. Because most items are packed flat, you can get them home easily, and assemble them yourself. This means we don't charge you for things you can easily do on your own. So together we save money… for a better everyday life.

Source: Used with the permission of Inter IKEA Systems B. V.

In addition, most customers found the IKEA shopping experience to be immensely appealing. Over the years IKEA had refined its retail approach, building off the success of its original flagship store in Stockholm. Although its stores tended to be cavernous—a typical outlet consumed 15,000 to 35,000 square meters—the store layouts were carefully designed. Upon entry, shoppers were gently coerced into a predetermined path through cheerfully decorated model bedrooms, kitchens, living

---

[6] Alexander von Vegesack, director of the Vitra Design Museum in Germany, who in 1999 mounted an exhibit on the history of IKEA, quoted in John Leland, "How the Disposable Sofa Conquered America," *The New York Times*, December 1, 2002.

rooms, and bathrooms. The atmosphere was always bright and inviting, and customers were free to lounge on the model furniture as they made their way through the store. Huge price tags adorned the goods, and color-coordinated cards offering design tips were displayed in information kiosks located throughout the store. In many ways, the stores resembled modern theme parks, with their childcare centers featuring large climbing structures and flamboyant playthings and their restaurants serving delicacies such as smoked salmon, Swedish meatballs, and lingonberry tarts. As Anders Dahlvig, IKEA's group president, put it:

> Many competitors could try to copy one or two of these things. The difficulty is when you try to create the totality of what we have. You might be able to copy our low prices, but you need our volumes and global sourcing presence. You have to be able to copy our Scandinavian design, which is not easy without a Scandinavian heritage. You have to be able to copy our distribution concept with the flat-pack. And you have to be able to copy our interior competence—the way we set out our stores and catalogues.[7]

Furniture Retailing in the United States

In the United States, furniture retailing accounted for $67 billion in sales in 2002.[8] The furniture market consisted of case goods (dressers, tables, dining room suites, bedroom furniture, etc.), upholstered furniture, bedding, ready-to-assemble furniture, and casual furniture. The first two categories (case goods and upholstered furniture) each accounted for roughly 45% of all furniture shipments; the other categories together accounted for the remaining 10% of the furniture market.

The market itself was highly fragmented; in 2002, the top 10 furniture retailers were responsible for just 14.2% of market share. (See **Exhibit 8** for details.) Within this market, there was a wide dichotomy between low-end and high-end retailers. The low end included general discount retailers such as Wal-Mart, office supply stores such as Office Depot, and discount warehouses such as Costco. (Wal-Mart was America's number one furniture retailer, in large part due to its huge retail footprint—it was the largest retailer in the world.) These general merchandise retailers tended to aggressively promote their furniture products on the basis of price; this cut-rate pricing meant that margins were extremely low in these channels. The low end also consisted of smaller shops that offered cheap furniture to price-sensitive customers; many of these shops targeted college students and others on a tight budget. The environment in these stores usually reflected their low-price focus—they were generally dreary and dingy, with haphazard product displays and inconsistent, poorly managed inventories. In all of the low-end channels, sales assistance tended to be poor to nonexistent, and product selections tended to be limited to utilitarian furniture that was either dull or altogether unattractive.

In contrast, most high-end specialty retailers offered luxurious store environments designed to conjure up aspirational images of affluence, prosperity, and comfort. These specialty retailers— which included both single-brand retailers such as Ethan Allen and Thomasville as well as multiple-brand retailers such as Jordan's Furniture—typically offered various payment options and easy credit to make it easier for shoppers to commit to a big-ticket item. Customers visiting these stores were usually serviced by high-touch sales consultants who could assist with measurement and product

---

[7] Quoted in Christopher Brown-Humes, "An Empire Built On a Flat-Pack," *FT.com* (London), November 23, 2003, p. 1.

[8] Based on data gathered by the American Furniture Manufacturers Association (AFMA), an industry trade group, as described in Amrit Tewary, "Household Durables," Standard & Poor's Industry Surveys, November 6, 2003.

selection; many stores also offered interior design services for consumers interested in a more complete home makeover.

Because the specialty retailers competed heavily on selection, they tended to boast of huge inventories; even the single-brand stores carried dozens of different styles. For example, it was not uncommon for these retailers to carry six to 10 styles of a given product type (e.g., American, Contemporary, Asian, European Country, etc.) and then to carry six to 10 *sub*-styles *within* each of these styles. This meant that a customer interested in a dining room table of the "American" style could choose from a variety of *sub*-styles such as Colonial American, American Country, Mission, Southwestern, and Shaker.

Specialty retailers also competed heavily on quality and service. With respect to case goods, salespeople were trained to educate consumers about quality markers such as grains of wood, construction techniques, and so on. Similarly, with respect to upholstered products, they were trained to educate consumers about the durability and longevity of different types of textures and fabrics, as well as inform them about add-on features such as stainproofing.

The salesperson's goal was always the same: To reassure customers that the furniture they were buying would last a lifetime. This was particularly important given that Americans were notorious for their reluctance to buy new furniture—the conventional industry wisdom was that most Americans hung onto their sofas for much longer than their cars and tended to "change their spouse as often as their dining room table, about 1.5 times in a lifetime."[9]

Finally, almost all furniture retailers (including many low-end retailers) offered delivery services, sometimes free of charge, sometimes for an additional fee. (Because furniture was usually sold in assembled form, it was difficult for customers to transport the furniture on their own.) As part of this delivery service, most retailers offered to set up the new furniture in the customer's home even if this involved rearranging existing furniture; they would also cart away the old furniture if the customer wanted to discard it.

By offering these delivery services, retailers could guarantee that, once customers purchased a piece of furniture, all they had to do was wait a few weeks for it to be delivered, at which time the furniture would be set up in their home without their having to lift a finger.

IKEA Invades America

It was in this context that IKEA competed in the United States. IKEA's success in America had not come easily. After opening its first U.S. store in Philadelphia in 1985, the company discovered that Americans did not like its products: apparently, its beds and kitchen cabinets did not fit American sheets and appliances, its sofas were too hard for American comfort, its product dimensions were in centimeters rather than inches, and its kitchenware was too small for American serving-size preferences. As one manager recalled, "People told us they were drinking out of the vases."[10] However, by paying close attention to customer complaints, IKEA had been able to address these problems, relying on market research to adjust its product lineup and merchandising.

---

[9] Christian Mathieu, external-marketing manager for Ikea North America, quoted in John Leland, "How the Disposable Sofa Conquered America," *The New York Times*, December 1, 2002.

[10] Ken Nordin, previously IKEA's sales and marketing manager for North America, quoted in John Leland, "How the Disposable Sofa Conquered America," *The New York Times*, December 1, 2002.

At the same time, IKEA had launched a high-profile advertising campaign designed to get Americans to take a more "commitment-free approach to furniture." Josephine Rydberg-Dumont, the managing director of IKEA of Sweden, explained:

> When you think of your own life, there's a time for several different lifestyles. That old, traditional stuff is making us feel the other way, that things can't change, that taking responsibility for your things is more important than taking responsibility for your life. It's O.K. to replace them, to get rid of them. We don't think we're going to live one way always. Our feeling is: It's just furniture. Change it.[11]

As an example, one IKEA ad campaign called "Unboring" had featured a series of television commercials poking fun at Americans' unwillingness to part with their furniture. The best known of these commercials had been an award-winning ad directed by Spike Jonz, a director best known for his film "Being John Malkovich." The spot (simply titled "Lamp") had opened with a discarded lamp sitting forlornly on the sidewalk in the rain and had concluded with an actor turning to the camera and saying, "Many of you feel bad for this lamp. That is because you are crazy. . . . "

By the mid-1990s, the company's fortunes in the United States had begun to improve, and from 1997 to 2001 the company was able to double revenues in the United States, from $600 million to $1.27 billion. By 2002, the United States was IKEA's third-largest market (after Germany and Britain, see **Exhibit 3**), and its 14 U.S. stores were servicing close to 30 million American customers a year (see **Exhibit 7**). As another indication of IKEA's success, the company's in-house restaurants were now the 15th-largest food chain in America.

As for its American customer base, IKEA described its typical shopper as the sort of person who traveled abroad, liked taking risks, liked fine food and wine, had a frequent-flier plan, and was an early adopter of consumer technologies such as Walkmen, laptops, and cell phones. (Incidentally, IKEA described its least likely customer as the type of person who collected guns.)[12]

Shopping at IKEA

For IKEA customers, shopping at IKEA required some preparation. As the company's Web site advised: "Be prepared. Make a list of anything you may need for your home. . . . Take measurements of spaces you want to fill with furniture. And be sure there's room in your car. You'll need it."[13]

Everything else customers needed to shop at IKEA was available at the store entrance: pencils, paper, tape measures, store guides, catalogs, shopping carts, shopping bags, and strollers. All of the stores were self-service, so if customers found smaller items they wanted, they could place the item in their shopping carts. If customers wished to purchase larger items, they could jot down the item numbers; they then needed to pass through the IKEA warehouse to pick up their flat-packed items before proceeding to checkout. (Self-serve trolleys were available to help customers carry their purchases from the warehouse to the checkout counter to the car.)

Customers were not only expected to transport their purchases home, they were also expected to assemble their purchases on their own. According to the Web site, "Picking up your purchases is an

---

[11] Josephine Rydberg-Dumont, managing director of IKEA of Sweden, quoted in John Leland, "How the Disposable Sofa Conquered America," *The New York Times*, December 1, 2002.

[12] Based on IKEA's internal market research, described in John Leland, "How the Disposable Sofa Conquered America," *The New York Times*, December 1, 2002.

[13] IKEA Web site: < www.ikea-usa.com>.

important part of IKEA's approach to customer involvement. Specifically, if you can do simple things like pick up your purchases and assemble them at home, we'll keep prices low."[14]

In terms of product selection, IKEA sold many types of furniture, but its style selection was limited according to the "matrix." As the Web site explained, "We don't have everything. We don't have the very extreme or over-decorated. We only have what helps build a home that has room for good living."[15] IKEA also sold every manner of household item, including dinnerware, rugs, lamps, and clocks. The company's total product range consisted of about 10,000 different products; many of these items featured bold colors and whimsical product names: Ticka alarm clocks, Fniss trash cans, and Bumerang clothes hangers.

If customers preferred to shop without their children, they could drop their kids off at the company-operated childcare facility on the way into the store. If they got hungry, they could stop by the IKEA restaurant for a lunch break. And if they needed assistance with shopping, they could stop by a sales desk and speak to an IKEA representative. The ratio of sales reps to customers was quite low, however, consistent with the company's self-service ethos.

Looking Forward

IKEA's goal was to have 50 stores in operation in the United States by 2013. Already, IKEA was the fastest-growing furniture retailer in the country and—excluding general merchandise retailers such as Wal-Mart, Office Depot, and Sam's Club—it was the seventh-largest furniture retailer in the United States.[16] (See **Exhibit 8**.) As one analyst put it, "Not only does IKEA have monster stores and great prices, it has also created a unique niche. It's the quintessential power retailer in America."[17]

Dahlvig added, "The more stores we build and the more we increase our market share, the more we have to find ways to appeal to a broader public. Scandinavian design and style is a niche and it is not to everyone's taste. But we don't want to be just another supplier of traditional furniture. Scandinavian design is what makes us unique. We have to find a balance."[18]

---

[14] IKEA Web site: <www.ikea-usa.com>.

[15] IKEA Web site: <www.ikea-usa.com>.

[16] Amrit Tewary, "Household Durables," Standard & Poor's Industry Surveys, November 6, 2003.

[17] Howard Davidowitz of Davidowitz & Associates, a retail consulting firm, quoted in Lisa Margonelli, "How IKEA Designs Its Sexy Price Tags," *Business 2.0,* October 2002.

[18] Anders Dahlvig, president of the IKEA Group, quoted in Christopher Brown-Humes, "An Empire Built On a Flat-Pack," *FT.com* (London), November 23, 2003, p. 1.

504-094   IKEA Invades America

Exhibit 1   IKEA Group: Sales Over Time

Year	Euros	Dollars
2003	€11.3 billion	$12.2 billion
2002	€11.0 billion	$11.9 billion
2001	€10.4 billion	$11.2 billion
2000	€9.5 billion	$10.3 billion
1999	€7.7 billion	$8.3 billion
~	~	~
1993	€3.8 billion	$4.1 billion

Source: Compiled from IKEA Web site: <www.ikea-usa.com>. FY runs from September to August. Exchange rate used: €1 = US$1.08.

Exhibit 2   IKEA Group: Sales by Region (FY 2003)

Region	% Sales
Europe	82%
North America	15%
Asia	3%

Source: Compiled from IKEA Web site: <www.ikea-usa.com>. FY 2003: September 2002 to August 2003.

Exhibit 3   IKEA Group: Top Five Sales Countries (FY 2003)

Region	% Sales
Germany	20%
United Kingdom	12%
United States	11%
France	9%
Sweden	8%

Source: Compiled from IKEA Web site: <www.ikea-usa.com>. FY 2003: September 2002 to August 2003.

Exhibit 4 IKEA Group: Store Locations (as of August 31, 2002)

Location	No. of Stores
Australia	4
Austria	5
Belgium	4
Canada	9
China	1
Czech Republic	3
Denmark	4
Finland	1
France	13
Germany	30
Hungary	2
Italy	7
Netherlands	9
Norway	5
Poland	7
Russia	2
Slovakia	1
Spain	3
Sweden	13
Switzerland	6
United Kingdom	11
United States	14

Source: Compiled from IKEA Web site: <www.ikea-usa.com>.

504-094

Exhibit 5   IKEA Group: Purchasing by Region (FY 2003)

Region	% Purchasing
Europe	66%
North America	3%
Asia	31%

Source: Compiled   from   IKEA   Web   site:
           <www.ikea-usa.com>.   FY   2003:
           September 2002 to August 2003.

Exhibit 6   IKEA   Group: Top   Five Purchasing Countries (FY 2003)

Region	% Purchasing
China	18%
Poland	12%
Sweden	9%
Italy	7%
Germany	6%

Source: Compiled   from   IKEA   Web   site:
           <www.ikea-usa.com>.   FY   2003:
           September 2002 to August 2003.

Exhibit 7   IKEA Stores in the U.S. (as of August 31, 2002)

Location	Opened	Size (m^2)
Philadelphia	June 1985	14,900
Washington – Woodbridge	April 1986	28,000
Baltimore	September 1988	18,700
Pittsburgh	July 1989	15,700
New Jersey – Elizabeth	May 1990	32,700
Los Angeles – Burbank	November 1990	22,500
New York – Long Island	May 1991	20,500
Los Angeles – City of Industry	May 1992	13,300
Los Angeles – Tustin	May 1992	13,500
Houston	July 1992	14,600
Los Angeles – Carson	November 1992	19,900
Chicago – Schaumburg	November 1998	40,000
San Francisco – East Bay	April 2000	25,500
San Diego	September 2000	17,700

Source: Compiled from IKEA Web site: <www.ikea-usa.com>.

Exhibit 8 Leading U.S. Furniture Retailers (ranked by 2002 sales of furniture and bedding)

Rank	Name
1	Wal-Mart
2	Rooms To Go
3	Ethan Allen
4	Levitz
5	La-Z-Boy
6	Office Depot
7	Sam's Club
8	Federated Department Stores
9	Berkshire Hathaway (incl. Jordan's)
10	Costco
11	Staples
12	Havertys
13	Value City
14	IKEA
15	Pier 1 Imports
16	JC Penney
17	Kmart
18	May Department Stores
19	Art Van
20	Rhodes
21	Office Max
22	Thomasville Home Furnishings
23	Lowe's
24	Big Lots
25	W.S. Badcock

Source: Adapted from Amrit Tewary, "Household Durables," Standard & Poor's Industry Surveys, November 6, 2003.

HARVARD | BUSINESS | SCHOOL

9-511-137
REV: JUNE 25, 2012

ELIE OFEK

ALISON BERKLEY WAGONFELD

Sephora Direct: Investing in Social Media, Video, and Mobile

Julie Bornstein, senior vice president of Sephora Direct, glanced through Sephora USA Inc.'s (Sephora) latest set of social media metrics as she waited for the elevator in the lobby of her company's headquarters in San Francisco, California. It was late in October of 2010, and she was heading up to the 32nd floor to meet with David Suliteanu, President and CEO of Sephora USA. Sephora was the largest prestige beauty specialty retailer in the world with nearly $2 billion of revenues from the company's stores in U.S and Canada as well as the Sephora.com website. Started in Europe in 1969, the company entered the U.S. in 1998, selling a wide range of cosmetic, fragrance, hair, and skin care products. Sephora was known for its vibrant stores that encouraged trial and experimentation.

As Bornstein stepped out of the elevator into the black and white striped hallway, she thought about the upcoming budget meetings with Sephora's parent company, Louis Vuitton and Moet Hennessy (LVMH). The Sephora Direct group was responsible for all of Sephora's direct marketing and digital initiatives, including Sephora.com and the Sephora Beauty Insider loyalty program. In 2008, Bornstein's team began to experiment on Facebook and with online videos, and in 2009 the team began making plans for mobile applications. By the summer of 2010 Suliteanu had authorized the creation of a new group within the Sephora Direct organization to focus on these new initiatives. Bornstein was hoping to double her budget in social media, video, and mobile for 2011, and she wanted Suliteanu to back up her requests for close to an additional $1 million dollars of funding. Suliteanu conveyed that he would support more funding if Sephora could "win" in this space, but it was up to Bornstein to determine what winning would look like for the company. Along those lines, Bornstein was contemplating how Sephora should measure the success of its digital efforts.

As Bornstein walked to Suliteanu's office, she glanced again at the weekly metrics sheet. She noted the rapid growth of Sephora "fans" on Facebook and the thousands of recent downloads of Sephora's new iPhone app. Bornstein felt good about the company's efforts to date, but she knew more opportunities lay ahead. Just last week she and her team talked about expanding their mobile offering, participating in social shopping programs, creating more videos, and increasing presence on Twitter. They also had the opportunity to pitch a promotional program for a new Jennifer Aniston fragrance launch using a variety of new media platforms. Bornstein thought about all of the directions they could pursue, focusing both on how to have the biggest impact and how to measure

Professor Elie Ofek and Alison Berkley Wagonfeld, Executive Director of the HBS California Research Center, prepared this case. HBS cases are developed solely as the basis for class discussion. Cases are not intended to serve as endorsements, sources of primary data, or illustrations of effective or ineffective management.

that impact to support additional funding. But even with additional funds, her team had only limited time and energy to dedicate to each of these programs, so they had to choose carefully. The meeting with LVMH was in ten days, and Bornstein was eager to discuss her ideas with Suliteanu.

Company Background

History

Sephora was started in France by Dominique Mandonnaud in 1969 as a single perfume shop. In 1979 Mandonnaud expanded to several stores, which were designed so customers could try multiple brands in an "assisted self-service" environment. Mandonnaud's retail concept represented a stark break from the traditional cosmetics retail model in which each prestige brand would commission its own sales representatives to push products onto shoppers, often in a department store setting at brand-dedicated counters. In 1993, Mandonnaud teamed up with investors to combine his stores with a perfume chain acquired from British retailer Boots PLC. Mandonnaud rebranded the combined set of stores under the Sephora name, derived from the Greek word for pretty (sephos) and the Biblical name Zipporah (Moses' beautiful wife). Mandonnaud continued expanding the chain, and several years later Sephora operated 54 perfume stores throughout France, representing 8% of the total French retail perfume market.[1] Sephora attracted the attention of luxury product group LVMH, which bought the company for $262 million in 1997.

U.S. Expansion

Under LVMH's ownership, Sephora expanded beyond perfume into other cosmetics and opened its first U.S. store in New York City in 1998. For the first few years, Sephora had difficulty getting products from Clinique, Estee Lauder, and Prescriptives, which were owned by Estee Lauder Companies and comprised 44% of the prestige beauty market in 1999.[2] These companies perceived Sephora as a niche player and would not distribute to Sephora stores located near department stores carrying the same lines. According to William Lauder, president of Clinique Laboratories and a board member of Estee Lauder Cos, "People will continue to shop at department stores because they offer trained salespeople who are knowledgeable about each brand."[3]

Given the reaction by some of the established brands, Sephora relied on less well-known brands to fill its shelves, and the company built relationships with hundreds of small cosmetic manufacturers. Sephora encouraged customers to try products in the stores, and multiple brands of similar product categories (e.g., lipsticks, eye shadow) were placed side-by-side to encourage experimentation. Sephora hired non-commissioned employees to guide consumers and answer questions, and over time, these employees were trained on all the different products.

All Sephora stores had a similar "look and feel" with black, white, and red as the dominant color theme for walls and displays, and employees ("cast members") dressed in these colors as well. (See **Exhibit 1** for store photos.) The stores played a combination of pop and alternative music that contributed to creating a fun, party atmosphere. The company attracted younger, hipper customers (referred to as "clients") than department stores. Suliteanu explained, "We told young women that it was OK to come in and try on make-up without buying anything. This was a new concept for cosmetic retailers, and it allowed us to grow the pie with customers who had never shopped for cosmetics before." Within several years of opening stores in the U.S., the bigger prestige cosmetic companies such as Estee Lauder and Clinique started supplying product to all Sephora stores. Suliteanu noted, "Over the years, the large public cosmetic companies like L'Oreal and Lauder have become much bigger supporters as our brand has grown both in size and credibility."

Sephora USA in 2010

By 2010, Sephora had nearly 1,000 stores in 23 countries, of which 450 were in the U.S. and Canada. Sephora had a retail presence in 36 states, with the majority of the stores in metropolitan areas and shopping malls. In 2006, Sephora entered into a retail partnership with JC Penney (a large chain of mid-range American department stores) in which Sephora became the exclusive beauty retailer inside JC Penney department stores. Approximately 200 of Sephora's U.S. stores were located within a JC Penney location. The company's headquarters were located in San Francisco where Bornstein managed a team of 75, organized into seven functional areas: customer relationship management, social media, acquisition and retention marketing, analytics, e-commerce, dotcom merchandising, and the company's call center. "Traditional" marketing and merchandising was run by Sharon Rothstein, senior vice president of marketing, who was based in Sephora's offices in New York City. (See **Exhibit 2** for management biographies.)

Sephora offered 288 brands, representing over 20,000 products, ranging from classic lines such as Lancome and Clinique to emerging brands such as Urban Decay and Too Faced. Sephora's products were considered prestige brands, which were perceived as more upscale than the mass market brands (e.g., Revlon, Maybelline) found at drug stores and supermarkets. Sephora carried nearly every large prestige brand except for Chanel and MAC Cosmetics. Sephora's pricing was often identical to that of department stores because U.S. beauty retailers tended to price prestige products at the manufacturer suggested retail price (MSRP). Promotions typically involved offering samples rather than discounting, although Sephora did offer two discount events each year to its loyalty card holders. Sephora also carried a host of private label products in nearly every category, some of which were priced below the prestige brands. Sephora's target market in 2010 was 25-35 year old women, many of whom "grew up" with the company. Bornstein noted, "This age group had an aspirational element, as the teenage girls looked up to this cohort and older women wanted to look 25-35 again."

Competitive Landscape

The U.S. beauty and personal care market was approximately $58.9 billion in 2009.[4] Sephora primarily competed with department stores such as Macy's and Nordstrom as well as single brand prestige beauty stores (e.g., MAC Cosmetics) and multi-brand specialty stores (e.g., ULTA Beauty). ULTA was the closest competitor to Sephora, as it operated nearly 400 retail stores in the U.S. Most of ULTA's stores were in "off-mall" locations (i.e., strip malls with 8-10 stores and easy parking), and included a full-service salon. The ULTA chain was started in the 1990s with an emphasis on discounted mass-market products, but the company added several prestige lines during the 2000s and positioned itself as a "beauty superstore" by the end of the decade boasting 21,000 products. In 2009, ULTA reached sales of $1.2 billion with $40 million of net income; analysts estimated 18% revenue growth for 2010 over 2009.[5] ULTA introduced an updated e-commerce site (ulta.com) in 2008, and had seven million members in its customer loyalty program in 2009.[6] ULTA did not have a distinct mobile offering in 2010. Bornstein described ULTA as a "fast follower" of Sephora. According to Karen Grant at NPD research, "The two chains go head to head among 25- to 34-year-olds, 29 percent of whom shop at Ulta, 30 percent at Sephora."[7] (See **Exhibit 3** for an article about ULTA.)

Sephora also competed with several large online merchants such as Amazon.com and Beauty.com, as well as hundreds of smaller sites. Two newer online companies included Birchbox, which delivered a curated box of samples to consumers each month in return for a monthly membership fee of $10, as well as Gilt Groupe, one of several growing companies that offered a limited set of luxury products at deep discounts during a short time window (known as "flash sales"). Sephora.com was the largest online prestige beauty website, capturing roughly 30% of the U.S. online market.

Sephora's Marketing Plan

Shortly after Rothstein arrived at Sephora in 2009, she worked with Bornstein to build a marketing plan for 2010. Key elements of the 2010 marketing mix included: store window merchandising, 32-page print catalogs sent to a portion of Sephora's Beauty Insiders three times a year, print advertising in magazines, a few direct mail pieces sent to Beauty Insiders, two major sales/promotions (one in April and one during the holiday season), and free gifts for Beauty Insiders. Rothstein and Bornstein talked regularly to coordinate messages, particularly around "animation" themes for the windows and Sephora's homepage. Rothstein explained, "Animations are one of the most important components of our marketing mix, they represent themes that form the basis of how we build our calendar. Our store window designs and site homepage bring our stores to life. Our CEO believes that our marketing image should start with the store experience, both offline and online." (See **Exhibit 4** for sample store window designs and print ads.)

In addition, Sephora spent millions on online search advertising (e.g., Google AdWords) by buying thousands of keywords for brands, products, and beauty related terms. Search advertising represented the single largest component of Sephora's marketing budget and was the largest source of new traffic to the Sephora website. Sephora was also looking into purchasing more online display advertising on sites such as Facebook. Email marketing to Beauty Insiders was also a key element of the marketing mix, and although the emails were not particularly expensive to send, Sephora spent millions on the entire Beauty Insider program. The 2010 plan had a modest amount of money (just shy of $1 million, representing under 5% of the total marketing budget) designated for social media, mobile and video, and those were the categories Bornstein hoped to double in funding in 2011. (See **Exhibit 5** for a breakdown of total media spending.)

Sephora Direct – Sephora.com and Beauty Insider

Sephora.com

Sephora.com was launched in 1999 with 100 brands, and within several months expanded to include all of the brands sold at any of the Sephora stores. The e-commerce site grew quickly into a sizeable business for Sephora, and it was projected to generate 15-20% of Sephora USA sales in 2010. The company appreciated the growth in online sales, as Sephora.com offered higher margins than a typical store due to lower overhead costs.

Approximately 3 million unique visitors came to the site each month, making Sephora one of the top 50 retail sites in the U.S. According to Comscore, on average in 2010, Sephora.com had 310,000 visits each day, and 11 page views per visit. The Sephora website offered sophisticated search functionality along with details about every product the company sold. (See **Exhibit 6** for Sephora.com trends from 2000-2010 and data about online beauty shoppers.) Sephora encouraged site visitors to purchase online by offering free shipping for orders over $50 and three free samples with every order. Suliteanu summarized, "Our web presence became an important part of our strategy. Our young clientele were going online and we needed to be there. The Sephora brand had been primarily about the physical experience, but we started to see the importance of the Internet as a forum where our customers could discover and learn."

Sephora Beauty Insider Program

Sephora USA introduced its Beauty Insider customer loyalty program in 2007. Suliteanu explained the rationale, "We wanted to know more about our customers, so we thought it would be helpful to introduce a CRM [customer relationship management] program. Most of these programs were set up around discounts, but our goal was to build our program around perks. We offered free samples to our Beauty Insiders and gave them "first looks" at new products. The program exploded and we had millions of sign-ups within the first year."

Clients were invited to join the Beauty Insider program when they made a purchase in the store or online, and all that was required was an email address, although clients were also asked for their birthdays. Bornstein commented, "Our store cast members [employees] get great training, and they really believe in this program. I've been in many stores and I have never seen a client buy anything without being asked to join our Beauty Insider program." Sephora offered one point for each $1 spent in stores or online. Clients could redeem points for a free gift at 100 and again at 500 points. Some opted to hold their points, hoping to redeem thousands of points for bigger gifts in the future.

Beauty Insiders typically received emails from Sephora once or twice a week, and a special offer on their birthday. Customers who spent more than $350 in a year were designated Very Important Beauty Insiders, also referred to as VIBs. VIBs were invited to special events at stores, received "deluxe" gifts and were given early access to products. VIBs were identified with a small icon when they posted questions or answers on the Sephora.com website.

By 2010, 15 million customers had signed up for the program; with 9 million considered "active members" (purchasing something from Sephora in the last 12 months). Approximately 80% of Sephora's sales came from Beauty Insiders. Bornstein commented: "One of the reasons the program works so well is that the beauty category lends itself to sampling, and our clients love to experience new products! We also make it really easy to join, and our clients see quick benefits. The program gives us a way to communicate frequently with our clients using our low cost email platform."

Sephora Direct - Social Media

Ratings and Reviews

Sephora's initial forays into social media began by enabling users to post product ratings and reviews on Sephora.com. In early 2008, Bornstein pushed to add this feature to the company's website even though there was internal concern about the implications of negative reviews. The direct team believed it was worth the risk because clients were asking for the feature, and research had shown that most people went online to rave about products rather than complain. In addition, the direct team believed that ratings and reviews could lead to desirable outcomes: improving site conversion from shoppers to buyers by providing confidence in a product's results, increasing traffic from online search results, keeping clients for longer durations on the site, reducing returns, lowering call center visits, and encouraging repeat visits. Moreover, other e-commerce sites such as Amazon.com already had active review boards, and some of Sephora's customers were posting reviews on these sites for products they had bought at Sephora.

Sephora contracted with a third party to build software that could be integrated into Sephora's website, and in September 2008, Sephora opened its ratings and reviews boards. The company publicized this new feature by emailing its Beauty Insiders, and within 24 hours Sephora had 32,000 ratings and reviews posted. Bridget Dolan, vice president of direct, recalled:

We were not sure what to expect when we opened the doors, and we were a little concerned that making reviewers sign in to our site would create a barrier to usage. However, within 24 hours we were flooded. Our clients were dying to talk with us and each other. Our third party contractor, Bazaarvoice, said they had never seen a response like this before. At first we thought we would need to read all the reviews before they went up on the site, but then we realized that would take months. We ultimately decided that our readers would let us know if there was an inappropriate review posted. So we did some basic electronic screening for inappropriate language and then let the reviews go up as written.

By September 2010 there were over 1 million product reviews posted, with an average rating of 4.2 stars (out of five). Dolan commented, "Some popular products have over 10,000 reviews. Initially I was surprised when someone wanted to write the 10,001th review, but I've learned that our clients love to share their personal experiences, particularly with a product they are passionate about."

Facebook

Sephora's experience with ratings and reviews gave the company confidence to expand its presence in other areas of social media. By late 2009, consumer behavior online had shifted, with 16% of all online time spent with social media,[8] representing exponential growth in a category that was practically nonexistent just three years earlier. Facebook was the largest and fastest growing social media site with over 500 million worldwide users and 53% reach in the U.S. in February 2010. In late 2008 Sephora created a Facebook "fan page" for its clients who wanted to follow Sephora and communicate with the company and each other online. Cathy Choi, director of social media, moderated the page and used Facebook's tools to add graphics and links. (See **Exhibit 7** for representative postings on Sephora's Facebook page.) Choi commented:

From the beginning, our clients were spending hours on our Facebook page, talking to each other and sharing their passion for make-up. We found that our clients were also talking directly to us through Facebook and they expected answers. Initially Julie, Bridget and I were spending our evenings and weekends reading all the posts and responding, until we formally pulled in some help from Sephora's call center support team. When clients asked questions about products, we often let other Facebook members answer. Sometimes we feel like we are playing the role of party hostess. We have super-users who are constantly responding to others, and we occasionally send them surprise gifts or emails to say "thanks." Many of the super-users are also our VIBs, and spend thousands of dollars at Sephora each year.

Dolan added:

We try to respond to questions directed to us, and we read all the client complaints and feedback. Clients use Facebook to let us know when we are out of products or if they had a bad experience at a store. Once we did an in-store promotional event and ran out of the tote bag give-aways. Our clients were not shy about using Facebook to express their frustration and it gave us a chance to respond in real-time to make it right! It is critical that we monitor our page carefully, or spammers can take over. Consumers can tell when a company's Facebook page is actively managed, and we are very careful about maintaining a consistent tone in our postings.

By late 2009 Sephora attracted over 300,000 fans to its Facebook page. The Facebook page also served as a forum for Sephora to do consumer research and get client feedback. In addition, early on, Sephora ran contests and occasionally offered promotions such as: "become a Facebook fan and get 10% off your next purchase." The company introduced a "Sephora Claus" sweepstakes for the 2009 holiday season that granted a product wish each day to one Sephora fan. Over 50,000 clients shared their wishes virally during the one month sweepstakes. Sephora tracked sales among contest entrants (through the use of a promotion code) and estimated the Sephora Claus program influenced over $1 million of sales. The sweepstakes also resulted in Sephora gift purchases from friends and relatives who could see the Sephora "wish list" of each entrant. Dolan estimated that Sephora incurred approximately $50,000 of direct costs to run the promotion, as well as staff time from various departments. The prizes were donated by brands that Sephora carried.

Sephora expanded its Facebook presence throughout 2010 and had nearly 900,000 fans by September 2010. (See **Exhibit 8** for fan growth). One industry analyst valued each Facebook fan at $3.60 based on the average number of messages a typical fan received and comparing that to the amount of paid online impressions needed to reach the consumer with the same number of messages.[9] Sephora teamed up with Facebook to participate in the launch of a new Facebook feature that allowed people to indicate what they "like" by clicking a "thumbs up" icon, and Sephora tracked its "likes" as a way to indicate client engagement. Bornstein's team constantly sought out fresh content and asked questions designed to elicit response. For example, Sephora posed questions such as "What color nail polish are you wearing right now?" and "Chocolate or Mascara, if you had to choose one, which would you give up?", many of which generated thousands of Facebook "likes" and comments. Bornstein's team was planning a new Facebook promotion for the holiday season in 2010 that had the potential to spread virally while also influencing sales. (See **Exhibit 9** for excerpts from a recent Sephora weekly dashboard highlighting client engagement on Facebook.)

Beauty Talk

Although the Sephora Direct team was pleased with its ability to engage with clients on Facebook, Bornstein, Dolan, and Choi expressed frustration with the lack of archival capacity on the platform. Dolan commented, "We find that clients ask the same questions over and over again, and there is not an easy way to save and query responses. Facebook is all about 'recency'—posts appear in the order they were logged." In addition, it was difficult to ask potentially embarrassing questions on Facebook because there was no way to mask a client's identity. Dolan described, "If a client has a question about acne or wrinkles, would she really want that question broadcast on Facebook under her real name?" Sephora did a survey in 2009 and found that 24% of respondents said they would be "very interested" in a central place to ask beauty questions of other Sephora shoppers on Sephora.com.

Consequently, the Sephora direct team decided to build its own question and answer forum with strong search functionality. The vision was to have a safe and private environment where clients could anonymously ask personal questions and get quick responses from Sephora experts or other members of the Sephora community. Dolan explained, "We asked ourselves, 'How can we make a more organized version of Facebook? How can we help users add more context to their questions?'"

Sephora contracted with a third party to design the Q&A engine as part of the Sephora.com website, and it was launched as a beta site called Beauty Talk in September 2010. With a few weeks of data, the Q&A forum showed promise, but it raised additional questions about the appropriate role of Sephora employees in moderating the discussion and answering questions. Dolan explained, "We struggle with finding the right balance between letting the clients share their own answers versus providing an expert Sephora opinion that could be perceived as biased."

Facebook did not make it easy to recognize "superusers" who answered a lot of questions. In contrast, Sephora encouraged Beauty Talk members to respond to queries by creating a "leaderboard" with 35 different levels. Users who posted frequently had a symbol identifying them as a "beauty master" or "beauty maven", while newer users might have a symbol labeling them as a "newcomer." VIB clients had a "VIB" symbol next to their names. Dolan explained:

> We found that our active responders like the recognition, and that was difficult to do on Facebook. We suspect that about 200 superusers will contribute the vast majority of the content

in our Beauty Talk forum, often posting on a daily basis. We couldn't possibly afford to staff up to supply all the answers provided by this group. We have other visitors that post a few times each month, but most of the visitors on Beauty Talk are passive viewers that benefit from the input of our superusers – they can read what is already there and get inspired to purchase.

The Sephora Direct team believed that Beauty Talk could become a key part of the Sephora experience; however it was unclear how to promote the forum and blend it with the Facebook site. Viewers could view and search among previously posted questions and answers on Beauty Talk; but that required leaving the Facebook site or using the two sites simultaneously. The direct team wondered how much they should try to move visitors from one site to the other, and any additional work on Beauty Talk would require more funding. Sephora found that early usage of Beauty Talk was not as high as the initial interest in ratings and reviews. Bornstein believed this was due, in part, to Beauty Talk being a more in-depth and less well-understood experience.

Twitter

Sephora started using Twitter in 2009. Anyone registered with Twitter could sign up to receive short (<140 characters) postings (referred to as "tweets") sent out by Sephora or anyone else that wanted to post on the Sephora news feed (referred to as "#Sephora"). By September 2010, approximately 100,000 users were "following" Sephora on Twitter. Sephora tended to use Twitter to spread news about promotions, contests, events, and other timely information. For example, Twitter was used as a communications channel during the Sephora Claus sweepstakes. Sephora clients also tweeted about Sephora when they came across a great product or a new promotion, or if they simply wanted to share thoughts about Sephora or make-up in general. (See **Exhibit 10** for sample Tweets.)

Online Video – YouTube

YouTube was the largest video sharing site in the world with 466 million users watching 73 billion minutes of video in 2009. Sephora began uploading videos to YouTube in 2007 and found that tens of thousands of users were watching its "how to" videos on topics such as "How to Get Perfect Brows" and "How to Curl Your Lashes." The most popular video – "How to Get Smokey Eyes" - attracted over one million views. In 2009, Sephora brought all company-produced videos together on an "official" Sephora YouTube channel that had nearly 100 videos that generated over 3 million views. In 2010 Rothstein's team added high-quality, professionally-produced videos into the mix about hot trends, and also produced short segments by founders of up and coming cosmetic companies.

A quick search for Sephora on YouTube in September 2010 also uncovered hundreds of user generated content (UGC) videos, many of which were filmed by Sephora clients in amateur settings. The topics of these videos ranged from makeup tutorials to showcasing recent shopping "hauls" (armfuls of products) from Sephora stores. Some of the UGC videos attracted as many viewers as the Sephora-produced pieces, which raised the question as to how Sephora should integrate the user content with its own professionally-produced videos. Dolan commented:

> Our Sephora videos help reinforce our positioning as an expert advisor, but professional videos can cost over $20,000 each to do well. We are evaluating our overall video strategy. What are we trying to accomplish? Should we mainly create functional "how to" pieces, or focus on brand-building? Are we using videos to broaden the Sephora community? How do we integrate our own videos with UGC segments? Our CEO would like to see us "own" the video category for personal care products, and we are trying to figure out what that means.

Rothstein added, "Like all aspects of marketing, videos are not formulaic, and it's difficult to predict which videos will take off. We always hear, 'Make something that goes viral.' That is easier said than done – it requires great content and ideas that are well-executed. We need to build enough videos to be noticed, but we can't be too scrappy as that doesn't fit our brand image."

Sephora Direct - Mobile

The proliferation of smart phones – phones with Internet and computing functions – gave retailers an opportunity to offer a rich mobile consumer experience. Bornstein noted the substantial increase in the number of users visiting Sephora.com from their phones in 2009. She also tracked data published by leading research companies that showed high projected levels of growth in both mobile usage and spending. According to comSCORE, mobile shopping rose from $396 million in 2008 to $1.2 billion in 2009, and was projected to reach $2.4 billion in 2010. Morgan Stanley projected that more consumers would access the Internet through mobile devices than personal computers by 2014. Bornstein was excited to capitalize on these shifts, "I started building a case for a Sephora mobile offering in 2009, and pushed even harder in early 2010 when I saw how mobile usage was taking off. We have an amazing website and amazing stores - I envisioned a mobile app that could serve as a bridge between the two." She believed a mobile app could help clients while shopping in stores by giving them the information they needed such as ratings and reviews to make purchasing decisions. In fact, Sephora had research showing that 25% of shoppers with smartphones used them during the buying process in 2009.

Bornstein spearheaded two major mobile initiatives in early 2010. The first was creating a version of the Sephora.com website optimized for mobile users (known as a "WAP" or "wireless application protocol"). The site could detect when a user tried to access Sephora.com from a smartphone, and that user would be shown a WAP version designed for a smaller screen. The WAP was launched in August 2010, and within days the team saw an increase in purchases from mobile phones.

The second project was the introduction of a custom-built Sephora iPhone application ("app") that users could download for free from Apple's App Store. Apps were platform specific and had to be downloaded, but then they remained on the user's device. Many apps enabled faster performance than a WAP and leveraged existing phone features such as camera and GPS functionality. The Sephora team opted to focus on building an app for the iPhone platform (instead of Android or Blackberry/RIM) because research indicated that iPhone penetration was highest among women, and Sephora's own data showed that over 90% of clients that accessed Sephora through their mobile devices in 2009 were using an iPhone or iTouch product.

Bornstein and her team created app specifications in early 2010 and hired a third party to build the iPhone application. (Third party prices for high-end apps ranged from $100,000 to $200,000.) Bornstein had a strong feel for what to have in the app based on her own experiences interacting with Sephora clients online and in stores. For example, she believed in-store users would appreciate the ability to look up their past purchases when replenishing cosmetics, and she thought shoppers could benefit from easy access to ratings and reviews. She believed a good mobile app would increase in-store purchases by providing instant answers to burning questions.

When designing the app, the Sephora Direct team noted the trade-off between functional elements such as a store locator feature, and playful brand-building elements such as interactive games. The direct group had some experience with an interactive app that had been designed for the Toki-Doki brand at Sephora. While users found it fun, it didn't seem to change purchasing behavior. This experience, and the desire to increase sales, led the team to launch the app with a focus on making shopping easier. When introduced in September 2010, the app had 12 primary areas: shop, shopping list, past purchases, new products, today's obsession, mobile offers, store locator, videos, ratings & reviews, gift registry, beauty advice and Beauty Insider. The app also let users scan the UPC codes of products in stores to learn more about them. (See **Exhibit 11** for an image of the Sephora app.)

Once the app was available through the Apple App store, users still had to find and download it. Bornstein commented, "Some retailers find it challenging to get their customers to download a specialized application, but we think our loyal clients will find us and be willing to download our app. We are fortunate that we have a way to reach our clients through our Beauty Insider program." Bornstein's team was also planning cross-promotions with Sephora stores, and the January window displays would showcase an image of the iPhone app in a custom designed black and white striped iPhone case. Users who downloaded the app would be eligible to receive a free iPhone case.

The early data seemed promising with 100,000 downloads of the iPhone app in the first few weeks. Bornstein hoped to have over 300,000 downloads by the end of the year, and estimated Sephora would generate several million dollars of sales through mobile devices in 2010. As soon as the app was available, consumer feedback started flooding in through Sephora's Facebook page, most of which was positive. A number of clients complained, however, that some of the app's features were slow to download. Clients also questioned Sephora's decision to focus solely on the iPhone and inquired when Sephora would have an app for Android and Blackberry/RIM devices. (In August 2010 it was announced that more Android phones were sold in the U.S. than iPhones, but iPhone still had higher penetration with women.) In addition, Apple had just introduced the iPad, a popular tablet computer, and Sephora was considering developing an app optimized for that format as well. Each of these apps would cost $100,000- $200,000 upfront, plus another $20,000-$30,000 of annual maintenance. The Sephora Direct team was weighing investments in these new mobile apps against adding more features to the current iPhone app or using the funds for other new opportunities.

New Opportunities in an Emerging Landscape

Sephora's early traction in social media, video, and mobile drew the attention of a broad spectrum of new media companies that wanted to partner with it. Bornstein explained, "We have been asked to participate in a number of online or mobile shopping platforms, and we are willing to do some experimentation if we can see the value for our clients." Some of the companies Bornstein considered partnering with included: Shopkick (a mobile platform to help consumers shop at multiple retailers through a single app), ShopSocially (a social shopping site where "friends help friends shop"), Foursquare (a mobile app to show friends where you are physically at any point in time), and Groupon (a group discounting site). (See **Exhibit 12** for details about these companies.) The Sephora direct team did trials with several of these companies, but it was not clear if any of the early partnerships would amount to anything, and there were so many start-ups attempting to play in these spaces. Bornstein commented, "I could see why a smaller retailer might want to use one of these new sites to generate traffic and sales, but we need to think hard about how much discounting we are willing to do for a program like Groupon, which typically requires products be discounted by 30-50%, or whether we want to spend the time and money to be part of group e-commerce apps if we can get a sizeable percentage of our clients to download our own app."

Many companies in the beauty industry also reached out to Sephora seeking cross-branding opportunities such as polls, surveys, and sweepstakes to be conducted through Sephora's Facebook site. Some of the companies offered to pay, but Sephora still found that it didn't have the resources to accommodate most of these requests. Dolan explained, "Each program we do involves, at a minimum, a designer, a writer, a programmer and a project manager. We are a small team and simply don't have time to work with all of the different brands that we sell at Sephora. We only want to pursue cross-promotional opportunities that drive traffic to our site and stores, and encourage consumers to purchase through Sephora. We have specific criteria to decide which programs we should or shouldn't do, but we also try to be opportunistic."

One interesting opportunity surfaced during the previous week. The actress Jennifer Aniston was planning to introduce a new fragrance in the coming months and was considering giving Sephora the exclusive rights to launch it in exchange for a high level of promotion. The direct team was intrigued by this opportunity, as they believed Aniston would appeal to their Beauty Insider community, but there was a lot that could be said for a more traditional campaign. Bornstein explained:

> We can propose a launch involving video, email, Facebook and Twitter. We are thinking of adding a donation to Jennifer's favorite charity each time someone indicates they "like" the new fragrance on Facebook. That said, Jennifer Aniston herself is not known for personally having embraced digital platforms, she does not have a Facebook page nor does she tweet; she is likely to be very familiar with traditional vehicles such as print and in store merchandising.

Conclusion

Bornstein was excited by all the opportunities these new technology platforms offered. Her team had experimented with different initiatives and had embraced Suliteanu's desire to "ensure they had enough in the petri dish to see what can work." As Bornstein prepared for the upcoming budget review, she had to plan her allocation among the different categories for 2011. (See **Exhibit 13** for a list.) But Bornstein realized it was also time to think more strategically about all of their programs. She was starting to craft a three year strategic plan for Sephora Direct – an effort that proved to be particularly challenging given the rapidly changing landscape in digital media. It was hard to predict which start-ups would gain substantial traction over the next year or two and how they would evolve, and new digital e-commerce ventures were being funded on a daily basis.

Bornstein thought about the priorities for her group and maintained that a core tenet of Sephora's strategy should involve deepening the company's connection with its Beauty Insiders. She explained:

> We know our clients shop at multiple stores, and we want to increase our share of their wallets. To do that, we need to make our brand come alive and inspire clients to buy more. Beauty is an affordable luxury, and theoretically there is no limit to the number of beauty products a client can own. We don't drive demand by frequent discounting, so we need to be more fun and innovative than our competitors. We have an opportunity to provide a wealth of expert advice through Beauty Talk. We are the number one beauty website, and we want to be the number one online destination for anything beauty related. We can see that clients who engage with us through Facebook and other channels purchase more than those who don't.

Bornstein believed that social media played an important role in helping Sephora listen to its clients. As Rothstein explained, "With the advent of Facebook, marketing has become a two way conversation." At times, Sephora specifically posted questions on Facebook under the headline: "Sephora Asks." While it was difficult to measure the effectiveness of using social media to hear from clients, Bornstein believed that it was always better to get feedback directly from clients – even if negative. Suliteanu commented, "We have learned that clients won't do anything they don't like." It thus made sense for Sephora to be in constant dialogue with its clients to find out what they *do* like.

A third aspect involved using these new technologies to acquire new clients. There were many regions in the country that did not have a Sephora store, so Sephora's online presence served as the primary way to invite new clients. Bornstein wondered if they should be doing more advertising through Facebook and YouTube to reach women who were not already part of Sephora's client base.

In addition to articulating the strategic goals for her team, Bornstein also thought about the ways she wanted to measure success. Her team tracked engagement level metrics such as number of Facebook comments, Twitter followers, and Beauty Talk posts. They also looked at the mobile usage data and noted where consumers tended to spend their time when using Sephora's iPhone app. Although these measures provided some sense of how well the social media initiatives were performing, Bornstein was still trying to identify the best way to calculate a more traditional return on investment (ROI). She reviewed various ROI frameworks proposed by industry experts and academics to enhance her own thinking on the matter. (See **Exhibit 14** for a sample framework.)

Nevertheless, both Suliteanu and Bornstein believed that ROI alone was not an adequate metric. They wanted to create a balance between building the brand and driving sales. Suliteanu explained, "Measuring success with these new media platforms only in terms of ROI would be putting us in handcuffs. Our social media initiatives help us create an emotional connection that is difficult to quantify. Our time horizon is long, and we are focused on the sensory experiences we create for our clients. For example, Sephora is opening a store in what used to be the meat packing district in NYC. It might seem crazy, but it helps keep our brand new and edgy." Bornstein expanded, "I see it as a win when Sephora gets invited to speak at top digital conferences or when we get mentioned as a social media leader in a news article. But these wins are meaningless if our efforts don't create more loyalty with our existing clients, allow us to acquire new customers, enable us to develop new value-add services, and ultimately help us to increase our sales."

The difficulty in calculating ROI made it challenging to determine optimal investment levels. Bornstein was hoping to double her budget for 2011, but it was unclear where that money would come from, and how the money if shifted to digital should be allocated. Rothstein shared her insights:

We have already reduced the number of new animations each year from 18 to 13, but stores remain the center of the Sephora experience. In recent years we have scaled back circulation of our catalogs to accommodate the new digital elements of our marketing plan. Should we further scale back our circulation and perhaps the length of our catalogs? At what point do we stop printing and mailing altogether? Everyone loves our catalogs. They showcase Sephora as a trend-setter and an expert, but can our videos do that as well? Media spending is not a perfect science, and both traditional media and new media play an important role.

As Bornstein sat down to talk with Suliteanu about her plans, she asked herself, "Are we thinking big enough?" Bornstein considered some recent remarks Suliteanu had made:

Sephora is big now, and the key word is balance. We have been watching companies like Starbucks, and it's clear that at some point the counterinsurgency they once embodied becomes the establishment, and we are conscious of that. The flip side of becoming more mainstream is that it's hard to be as cool and innovative. I feel a kindred spirit with brands such as Apple and Nike. We spend more time on how to be unique and unexpected than almost anything else. We have a wonderful set of loyal clients, but we don't want to be complacent. We have to stay one step ahead of Mrs. Jones. We recognize that our clients can go anywhere else at any time, and the minute we stop providing a special experience we risk losing them.

She realized that simply pouring more money into various digital avenues was not necessarily the right answer. It was important to first articulate her team's objectives with respect to these new communication platforms and then come up with effective ways to achieve and measure them.

Exhibit 1   Sephora Store Photos

Source: Sephora.

Exhibit 2   Sephora Executive Bios

David Suliteanu, President and CEO of Sephora USA. Suliteanu joined Sephora in July 2000 from Home Depot, where he was Group President/Diversified Businesses from 1998 to 2000. In that position he was responsible for the Expo Design Center, Home Depot's upscale remodeling and décor showrooms, and Villager's Hardware, smaller-format hardware stores. Prior to that, Suliteanu spent seven years at Macy's East, the largest division of Federated Department Stores. Before that, he held several retail positions, including: Senior Vice President/General Merchandise Manager of Foley's in Houston; Regional Vice President of Stores at Sanger Harris in Dallas; and Vice President/Store Manager at Macy's West in LA. Mr. Suliteanu received a B.A. in economics from Stanford University.

Julie Bornstein, Senior Vice President, Sephora Direct. Before joining Sephora in 2007, Bornstein served as the general manager of Urban Outfitters Direct where she led the growth of the web and catalog division into a highly productive and profitable direct business. Before Urban, Bornstein served as vice-president of ecommerce for Nordstrom from 2000-2005, joining as Nordstrom launched its first website to grow the business from $12M to over $350M, and overseeing merchandising, marketing, creative and customer experience for the website and catalog. Bornstein started her career in merchandising at DKNY, and also worked in business development at Starbucks. Bornstein received her BA and MBA from Harvard University.

Sharon Rothstein, Senior Vice President, Marketing. Rothstein joined Sephora in May 2009. Prior to Sephora, Rothstein served as Senior Vice President, Global Marketing and Merchandising at Godiva Chocolatier, the world's leading super premium chocolate brand. Prior to Godiva, Rothstein was Senior Vice President, Global Marketing with Starwood Hotels and Resorts. In earlier roles, she served as Chief Executive Officer of WorldSpy.com, an e-commerce retailer, and Senior Vice President, Marketing and Entertainment of Discovery Zone. Earlier in her career, Rothstein worked at both Nabisco and Procter and Gamble. Rothstein earned her Bachelor of Commerce (Honors) from University of British Columbia and her MBA from the Anderson School of Business at UCLA.

Source: Sephora.

Exhibit 3   Excerpts from News Article about Ulta from *The New York Times* (2009)

Can Ulta Muss Up Sephora's Makeup?

Until recently, Alessandra Salvatore, 27, happily made a beeline to the nearest Sephora when she craved an $18 lip plumper of her favorite scent, Giorgio Armani's Emporio She. But because Sephora with its Parisian pedigree doesn't sell drugstore makeup, Ms. Salvatore required another stop to grab a $7.29 Maybelline Full N' Soft mascara. That was before she moved from Briarcliff Manor, N.Y., to Charlotte, N.C., and discovered Ulta, a national chain of beauty stores that brings together designer fragrances, drugstore staples, salon-only hair products, as well as a growing selection of prestige cosmetics like Benefit and Smashbox. Cavernous enough for 21,000 products and cut-and-color hair salons, Ulta stores are often in strip malls, a convenience she appreciates.

Sephora may have pioneered the concept of glitzy stores as playgrounds where women could dab and smear prestige lipsticks and face creams. No longer was a salesclerk a gatekeeper to the makeup, nor a cheerleader for the single brand that paid her commission. Instead, roving experts helped as needed. Now Ulta, with 331 stores nationwide, is trying to go Sephora one better. It offers inexpensive beauty staples found at the likes of Target, along with easy access to prestige treats that used to be trapped behind glass. There are also hair salons in each Ulta store and stylists to help navigate the rows of professional hair products. Lyn P. Kirby, Ulta's chief executive, likes to call the company a "category killer," as if she wants to tear down the walls segregating L'Oréal in pharmacies from high-end skin care in department stores and beauty chains.

"They have a critical mass of prestige brands," said Liz Dunn, an analyst at Thomas Weisel Partners, adding: "Part of the off-mall appeal is convenience. They're trying to target the time-starved woman who wants an easy shopping experience." Critics say Ulta is hardly within Sephora's universe. Until Ulta stores offer beloved standards like Clinique Dramatically Different lotion and more adventurous niche makeup brands, they say, it cannot be considered one-stop shopping.

Ulta, which used to be a discount retailer with a schlocky look, has added sleek stores at a clip. It opened 65 stores in 2008, including its first urban locations, a four-floor showpiece in Chicago and a behemoth in Miami. Although luxury brands can be leery of being sold under the same roof as, say, CoverGirl, Ulta is having some success luring them. Lorac, a fresh-off-the-red-carpet cosmetics line created by the makeup artist Carol Shaw, has been in Sephora. Lorac arrived at Ulta in 2008. When Ulta came courting, David Hirsch, part of the senior management team at Lorac, said they worried about "downmarketing" the brand. But he soon grew convinced that women don't enjoy their high-end splurges any less just because Maybelline is sold a section over. "It's sort of like a Baskin-Robbins," he said. "There's nonfat yogurt but there's the good stuff, too." For some, convenience is paramount. "When my wife walked into Ulta for the first time, she thought, 'I can knock off a couple of things here,' which you can't do at Sephora."

Many beauty shoppers are fickle when it comes to store allegiance, said Karen Grant, the vice president for beauty at NPD, a market research firm. The two chains go head to head among 25- to 34-year-olds. Meanwhile, Ulta has an edge with women older than 44, who "tend to be more loyal," Ms. Grant said, because "Ulta rewards that loyalty" with savings. After landing a deal on a curling iron, Emily Veitia wrote a customer review on Yelp.com: "Ulta, you are Sephora's nemesis!"

But in a telephone interview, Ms. Veitia lamented that Ulta "felt a little bit like a beauty supply store." She would rather "save up some money and go to Sephora" she said, because "it's more on top of the times." Some of Sephora's niche brands include Living Proof No Frizz hair care, Tarte cosmetics, Make Up For Ever and Josie Maran. None of which Ulta carries.

Ulta's personality is best described as "approachable and in style," Ms. Kirby said in an interview. "We are not about intimidating. Sephora's black and white isn't approachable." The peachy color of Ulta's awnings and bags is an expression of that sentiment.

Annie Vazquez, a freelance journalist in Miami, likes that she can get two of her Matrix Biolage color care shampoos for $20 at Ulta, whereas elsewhere she has paid $25 a bottle. She is not yet ready to make the store her one-stop beauty destination, not until it carries the Laura Mercier tinted moisturizer she can't go without. For now, her allegiances are divided. "Sephora, it's not that it's pretentious or anything like that," she said, "but Ulta is more down to earth, and sometimes when you're on the go, and we all are, you just want to get there, get what you need, and go."

Source: Catherine Saint Louis, "Can Ulta Muss Up Sephora's Make Up," *The New York Times*, July 23, 2009, http://www.nytimes.com/2009/07/23/fashion/23Skin.html, accessed April 29, 2011.

Exhibit 4   Sephora Sample Window Designs and Print Advertisements

<u>Sample Store Fronts</u>

Sample Print Advertisements

Source: Sephora

Exhibit 5 High Level Break-down of Sephora Media Spending

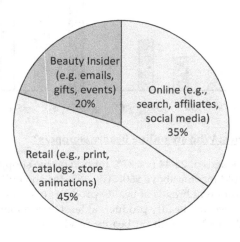

Note: Search advertising represented the bulk of the online category.

Source: Sephora.

Sephora Direct: Investing in Social Media, Video, and Mobile   **511-137**

Exhibit 6   Sephora.com Website Statistics and Online Beauty Shopping Trends

<u>**Sephora Website Visits (% represents growth in visits over previous year)**</u>

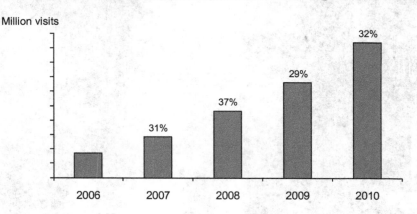

<u>**Net Sephora.com Sales Growth Trend ($)**</u>

Bars represent growth trend in $ sales in 2000-2009 and estimated sales for 2010.

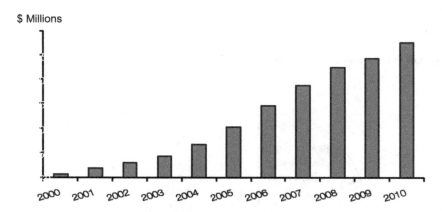

<u>**Online Beauty Shopping Trends: Who are online beauty shoppers?**</u>

- **43%** are between the ages of 25-44 (vs. 37% for non online shoppers)
- **50%** have a household income above $60K (vs. 46% for non online shoppers)
- **20%** use 6 or more different brands of beauty products (vs. 10% non online shoppers)
- **48%** use the web to research beauty products at least once a month
- **60%** spend more than $25/month on beauty products (vs. 40% among consumers who don't shop online)
- Each month **20%** use search engines to shop for and research beauty products
- **Twice** as likely to read beauty magazines

Source: Sephora and Google and Compete Beauty Webinar, "Searching for Beauty Shoppers," May 5, 2009.

Exhibit 7   Sephora Sample Facebook Page Postings

Ashley Klitzke

Alot of my friends who are VIBS or Beauty Insiders have recieved a card in the mail for a free bare escentuals sampler with 25 dollar purchase. I did not recieve one and I'm a VIB, will I be able to simply mention this offer at the counter and recieve the samples?

4 hours ago · Like · Comment

👍 Brande Patterson likes this.

 Kent N Valerie Brower I didn't either and I've been a VIB since Jan. Not cool!

3 hours ago · Like

 Sephora Hi ladies. Yes, you can take advantage of the offer by mentioning it at the store or calling 🇺🇸 ▾ **1-877-SEPHORA** 🌐 for online orders. It is available while supplies last with a $25 purchase. Hope that helps!

3 hours ago · Like

 Olga Lopez Pinar i didnt get an email either

2 hours ago · Like

Write a comment...

Kelly N   ✕

I love the sephora lux matte bag wish they'd give it out more often. SO useful and not cheap quality.

June 16 at 5:26pm · Like · Comment

👍 Sephora likes this.

💬 View all 2 comments

Write a comment...

Jodi DiBiasi

I haven't gotten an email in a while- anyone know what promo codes are still valid right now?

June 16 at 7:06pm · Like · Comment

 Sephora Hi Jodi. We just sent you a message to help fix your e-mail subscription. Click here for our current promotional offers: http://bit.ly/mxwSuj. Enjoy!

June 16 at 7:39pm · Like

Write a comment...

Tinker Belle

Thank you so much Sephora for making a highlighting powder that's not yellow toned! I'm cool toned and they look funny on me. Everyone should try Sephora highlighting compact powder in rose! Gorg!

June 16 at 2:02pm · Like · Comment

👍 3 people like this.

💬 View all 9 comments

Source: Sephora (from Facebook).

Sephora Direct: Investing in Social Media, Video, and Mobile   511-137

Exhibit 8 Sephora Facebook Statistics (September 2008 – September 2010)

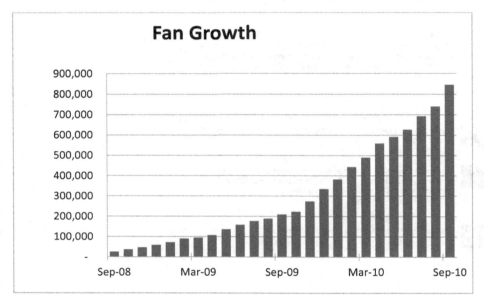

Source: Sephora.

Exhibit 9 Excerpt from Sephora Weekly Dashboard (September 2010)

- **812k** Total Facebook Fans in September (month to date)
- **71.8k** new fans September month to date (47.7k new fans in Aug)
- **Best Update by Sales:** VIB offer $10.5k
- **WEEKLY HIGHLIGHTS**
  - **1 Quick Question**
    - Lipstick or Lipgloss – which would you give up: 1734 comments, 484 likes
    - What's your beauty obsession: 725 comments, 311 likes
    - What is your perfect red shade: 214 comments, 261 likes
    - Ask Michelle Phan a question: 194 comments, 736 likes
    - Match your eye makeup to outfit: 953 comments, 475 likes
  - **Bobbi Brown Launch**
  - **Ustream for MAKE UP FOR EVER (MUFE) boutique in SOHO**
    - First live streaming video event
    - Over 1200 Fan interactions
  - **Red Haute Mosaic FB application**
    - Clients uploaded image of themselves with red lips into photo mosaic
    - 3773 Installed users
    - Over 200 Client stories shared
  - **TEMPTU quiz**
    - Brand interaction through quiz; 738 quizzes taken

Sephora Status Update Calendar and Results for September 2010
(highlighting indicates the postings that generated the highest level of engagement)

date	topic	comments	likes	Imp
1-Sep	1QQ Red Lip	214	261	718,019
2-Sep	Bliss Rollerball GWP	55	336	712,819
3-Sep	Michelle Phan FNO	194	736	693,062
6-Sep	1QQ	953	475	770,803
7-Sep	FNO	54	480	706,168
8-Sep	Paco Rabanne	82	249	665,647
9-Sep	Stilla Smudge Stick	75	443	656,742
10-Sep	N/A			
13-Sep	Choose 1 of 6	49	173	485,410
14-Sep	New York Fashion Week	39	314	685,719
15-Sep	Temptu Quiz	120	508	683,956
16-Sep	FNO video	47	312	609,821
17-Sep	1QQ	717	312	651,092
20-Sep	Bobbi Brown	206	397	503,745
21-Sep	Murad Clean Scene GWP	38	151	476,113
22-Sep	Dior Video	67	582	779,752
23-Sep	1QQ	1734	484	666,180
24-Sep	VIB Choose 1 of 3	144	744	844,718
27-Sep	Extra VIB Appreciation Bags	88	233	563,494
28-Sep	BeautyTalk Eary Access	60	414	852,918
29-Sep	YSL FNO vid	52	379	739,709
30-Sep	MUFE Boutique opening	113	828	809,576
30-Sep	USTREAM	215	52	730,020

Source: Sephora.

Exhibit 10   Sample Tweets with #Sephora

Source: Sephora.

Sephora Direct: Investing in Social Media, Video, and Mobile   511-137

Exhibit 11   Sephora iPhone App Homepage Design

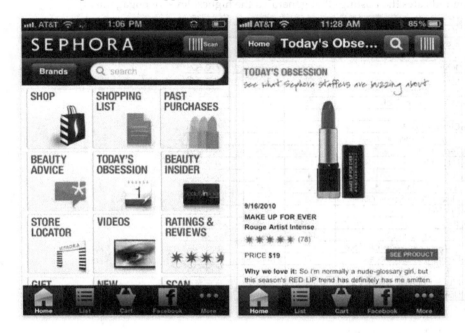

Source: Sephora.

Exhibit 12   Description of Mobile and Social Media Companies

Foursquare was a location-based social networking site that used software for mobile devices. The service was available to users with GPS-enabled devices such as smart phones. Users were rewarded for "checking in" at venues when using the mobile app or text messaging by receiving points or badges.

Groupon was a deal-of-the-day website for major markets in the United States. Users could sign up to receive daily emails about specific deals (typically for things to do, see, eat, or buy) that were only valid on that particular day. The company had 35 million registered users in September 2010.

Shopkick was a mobile application that gave consumers rewards and offers when they walked in to a participating store. Consumers could earn "kicks" by opening up the mobile app and "checking in" to the store or by scanning items in the store. Kicks could be redeemed for rewards.

Shop Socially (Shop Social.ly) was a social shopping platform based on the premise that buying decisions should be influenced by friends. The company helped users ask friends for recommendations when they were buying something, and users could share their own purchases and expertise to help friends shop.

Source: Casewriter research.

Exhibit 13   Proposed Categories for Sephora's 2011 Social Media, Video and Mobile Budget

Budget Category	Description/ Programs	2011 Budget Allocation
Video Production		
Video/YouTube Advertising		
Video Contest		
Facebook Development		
Holiday/Viral Promotions		
Social Partnerships		
Mobile		
Store Kiosks		

Source: Sephora.

Sephora Direct: Investing in Social Media, Video, and Mobile   511-137

Exhibit 14   Example of a Third Party Social Media Evaluation Framework

Social Media ROI = (Derived Value – Investments) / Investments

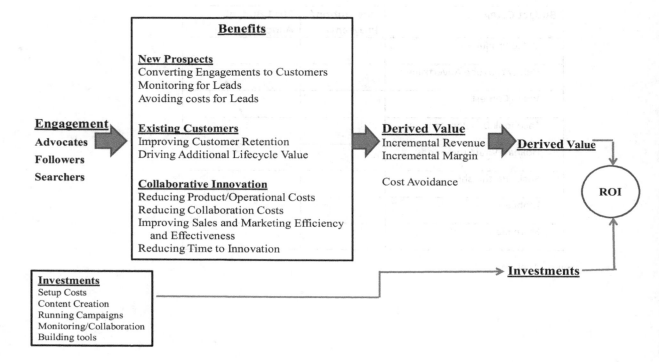

Engagement Level	Description	Typical conversion rate from a digital/social engagement to purchase*
Advocates	Actively participate in interactive threads and post comments frequently	2.25%
Followers	Registered as followers on company's social platforms (such as a follower on Twitter or Blogs, or a fan on Facebook)	1.125%
Searchers	Monitor and listen to social media streams for items of interest; scan online resources to find relevant information	0.75%

*By comparison, click through rates for online banner ads are assessed at 0.1-0.2% on average, with conversion to purchase post click some fraction of that)

Source: Adapted from Tom Pisello, http://www.contentmarketinginstitute.com/2011/01/roi-social-media-marketing/, accessed June 16, 2011, and Dave Chaffey, "Display advertising clickthrough rates" January 10, 2011, http://www.smartinsights.com/blog/internet-advertising/display-advertising-clickthrough-rates/, accessed June 20, 2011.

Sephora Direct: Investing in Social Media, Video, and Mobile

Endnotes

[1] http://www.referenceforbusiness.com/history2/73/Sephora-Holdings-S-A.html, accessed March 24, 2011.

[2] Diane Seo, "Sephora Applies a Bold Stroke to Cosmetic Sales," *Los Angeles Times*, February 11, 1999, http://articles.latimes.com/1999/feb/11/business/fi-7008, accessed March 24, 2011.

[3] Ibid.

[4]   Euromonitor,   http://www.icis.com/Articles/2010/04/19/9350061/sustainability-helps-cosmetics-companies-beat-the-recession.html, accessed May 31, 2011.

[5] Brian Tunick, Ike Boruchow, Jr., "Ulta Salon, Cosmetics & Fragrance, Inc.," J.P. Morgan, January 31, 2011. P. 3.

[6] ULTA 2009 10-K, published March 31, 2010.

[7] Catherine Saint Louis, "Can Ulta Muss Up Sephora's Make Up," *The New York Times*, July 23, 2009, http://www.nytimes.com/2009/07/23/fashion/23Skin.html, accessed April 29, 2011.

[8] Data from Sephora, originally from a Morgan Stanley report.

[9] Based on study by Vitrue, posted online at: http://www.rcubed.co.za/blog/measuring-value-of-a-facebook-fan/, accessed on June 16, 2011.

H A R V A R D | B U S I N E S S | S C H O O L

BRIEF CASES

9-913-545

REV. OCTOBER 23, 2013

JOHN A. QUELCH

JAMES T. KINDLEY

Brannigan Foods: Strategic Marketing Planning

On a rainy New Jersey morning in November, 2012, Bert Clark, vice-president and general manager of Brannigan Foods' Soup Division, scanned his in-box for new messages. He saw that each of his four key managers had digested analyst Julian DeGennaro's annual "State of the Soup Industry" summary report (**Exhibit 1**) and had responded to Clark's request that they recommend their best investment bets for the division. (See **Exhibit 2** for Brannigan's product lines.) In Clark's 16-year career with Brannigan he couldn't remember a tougher, more complicated challenge than the one he now faced. The soup industry had been in steady decline for several years, and the division's sales, market share, and profitability had slipped for the last three.

Clark skimmed his managers' emails, hoping for new concepts and fresh, timely arguments. Each manager had indeed sketched a proposal "most likely to turn the division around." Unfortunately, the proposals bore no resemblance to each other. Clark decided to revisit DeGennaro's report and then consider each proposal in depth.

The Soup Industry in 2012

As he reviewed DeGennaro's findings, Clark was particularly concerned about the major consumer trends affecting the sale of soup. Condensed and ready-to-eat (RTE) soups were still a staple in most diets in the United States. However, the growing concern about health and obesity had led to a reduction in processed foods in general and products with high sodium content in particular. This trend was especially pronounced among the so-called baby boomer generation (born between 1946 and 1964), the first wave of which was now entering retirement. This group was the largest and most brand-loyal segment of soup consumers, as the report indicated. Products had to be targeted to them. However, this had serious long-term implications for Brannigan as it also needed to engage younger generations of consumers. Clark felt, in fact, that this was one of the most pressing needs for the company.

The other critical trend lay in the U.S. population's increasing desire, especially among working mothers, for fast, simple meals. Clark needed to win this consumer from a wide array of strong competitors. The rapidly increasing sales of premade "deli soups", dry-mix soups, and microwavable packaged soups, while not nearly as large as the canned soups category, was consistent with this trend.

Clark noted with some satisfaction that Brannigan maintained the leading market share of shelf-stable soups and that three years of price increases had helped to keep profit from declining as much as sales. His division was responsible for more than half the profits of the company's U.S. divisions (40% of sales) and he wasn't going to back off his growth goals of increasing those profits by 3% next year.

Clark's Challenge to His Reports

Could his team help him come up with a focused, coherent plan for growth? Clark thought back to the four strategic challenges he had presented to them:

1. Can new benefits be added to the current lines to increase their growth and profitability?

2. Does an acquisition make sense to strengthen or diversify our lines?

3. What new products might we develop internally that address the health and convenience trends? Or do we have enough new products already that can reverse the slide if they are properly marketed?

4. What marketing strategy should be employed in reference to each of the above and how much should be put behind the drive for next year versus what we should invest for our long-term objectives?

Clark wasn't certain that these four options were exhaustive, but they were sure to surface the best ideas his team could come up with. To anchor their thinking in financial reality, he had also included his preliminary forecast for sales, marketing costs, and net income for next year (Exhibit 3).

Now Clark read through the messages from the four people he most depended upon:

- Srikant Tipha, Director of the Simple Meals unit;

- Claire Mackey, Director of Finance and Planning;

- Anna Chong, Chief Innovation Officer; and

- Bob Pugh, Director of Sales and Marketing.

Invest in the growing sectors
From: tiphas@brannigan.com
To: clarkb@brannigan.com

Hi Bert

JJ's Report is spot-on. We need to continue to reinforce the strategy we've been following in the past few years by upping the investments in the on-trend winners in the growing categories of dry soups, healthier soups, and fast meals. Increasing our investment in these soups will have a positive impact on our brand image, bringing it into the 21st century, as well as driving long-term growth.

I believe the *Fast & Simple* meal-in-a-pouch soups line that we purchased from Annabelle's Foods several years ago is finally on the right track. Sales are growing at 12% per year because the line addresses the needs of working mothers and professionals looking for a fast but healthy meal.

The low-sodium *Heart Healthy* soups introduced several years ago are also gaining traction and market share, as shown in the report, as they are well positioned to address the concerns of over-50 consumers.

The dry soups category is also expanding. We only have a few offerings at this point, but they are very promising. The dry soup mixes also help us address the retailer's desire to squeeze more profit from our shelf space. Two dry mix packs can be sold in the space of one can, increasing the sales potential by 180%.

Here's a plan:

1. Reinforce awareness of our new items and induce trial by increasing the advertising investment in the *Fast & Simple* soup meals and the *Heart Healthy* soup line. We're somewhat behind our competitors in this space, but our retailer and consumer market strength should allow us to grow market share rapidly, if we spend appropriately.

2. Provide promotional couponing and sampling of the hot new flavors, in particular the dry mix Gazpacho and the Teriyaki Beef *Fast & Simple* meal. The Gazpacho will provide an added bonus of increasing sales during the warmer months, decreasing seasonality. The Teriyaki Beef positions us in the fast growing Asian soups category.

3. Continue to promote dry soups, even if they cannibalize Ready-to-Eat (RTE) soups.

I'm proposing an increase in our advertising and promotion spending of $18 million (the numbers below are based on the forecast you provided). Exhibit 3 This should help stop the slide in sales and market share, although it will reduce next year's profits. We should make this move for the long-term revitalization of the brand and to gain leadership in the growing categories.

	Present division sales this year	with additional advertising spending next year
	2973	2954* ($2913 forecast)
Adv promo	178	188
Op income	295	297

*Half my proposed sales increase comes from the Heart Healthy soups and half from the other items listed above.

Let's talk this over when convenient.

Srikant Tipha
Category Manager – Simple Meals, Heart Healthy Soups, Dry Soups

Srikant had done a good job integrating *Annabelle's* products into Brannigan line in the face of some serious challenges. His "healthier" new products also seemed to be gaining traction. But Clark worried that spending more on these small lines might not produce the sales Srikant projected. He made a note to ask Srikant what sales had to be hit to reach breakeven on the additional advertising spend. Clark also sensed that due to the competitive activity in these areas that Tipha's products had lower gross profit than the core products. Clark also feared that these "on-trend" initiatives may never become large categories for Brannigan's. Most consumers knew they should eat more healthy foods, but with close to 70% of the US overweight it was obvious that few actually were changing their eating habits.

Clark was also concerned about having to revise profits down for 2013 if he followed Srikant's advice. He knew that CEO John Wilson was going to demand an airtight justification for it. Wilson was under increasing pressure from the board and the stockholders and he would probably be unwilling to give up any profit. Clark made another note to ask Srikant what sales had to be for operating income to equal his projections for 2012.

Clark's also thought that chasing the trends may not amount to a viable long term strategy in spite of Srikant's comments to the contrary.

He picked up the next email.

Acquire product lines to complement the core in growing sectors

From: mackeyc@brannigan.com
To: clarkb@brannigan.com

Bert:

The DeGennaro report indicates that a number of small competitors are offering healthier and more convenient soups, as well as flavors rapidly gaining in popularity, such as Mexican and Southeast Asian, where we have little presence. Here are several companies that we should consider acquiring to bring Brannigan into these categories. I particularly like *Red Dragon Foods*.

Roarin' Cajun Foods
Baton Rouge, LA. Key product: ten-bean dry mix soup. MSG and sodium free. Key customer: Whole Foods.
$18 million sales. Estimated EBITDA for 2011: $2.8MM
Would provide entry into WF if we do not use the Brannigan's brand.

Red Dragon Foods
Los Angeles. Key products: Southeast Asia and Chinese soups. Key customers: Safeway, Ralph's chains.
$36 million sales. Estimated EBITDA:$4.2MM
Would give us entre into Asian flavors and has the potential for numerous additional products. Brannigan's brand could be incorporated reducing the advertising and promotional investment required by 55%.

Brothers Gourmet
Rhinebeck, NY. Upscale soups centered on classic "deli-like" products such as Brooklyn Chicken Noodle. Key customer: Pathmark
$12 million sales. Estimated EBITDA: $3.4MM
Would bring higher priced, higher margin items into our line. Brothers brand should likely be maintained.

Speculating, the price for any of these would likely be in the six to seven times EBITDA range. Interest rates are about 4% now so debt service would be low and would not impact profit significantly. Of course, with the recent down year, any negative impact on profit is going to be scrutinized. My best guess is that any of these acquisitions will add around 1.5 to 3.5% to our sales within five years if we invest appropriately in marketing them. Cannibalization is hard to project. Red Dragon, as an example, should cannibalize less than 0.3% of our total sales if we were to acquire it and keep its brand.

Let me know if you would like to begin due diligence on any of the above companies…

Claire Mackey, Director of Finance & Planning

Clark had vivid memories of the acquisition of *Annabelle's Foods* soups' division five years ago. It was supposed to accelerate the growth of the division's *Fast & Simple* category, but folding *Annabelle's* line into existing offerings had been a nightmare. Its plant was plagued with production miscues as efforts to take *Annabelle's* products into major retail channels overwhelmed its capabilities. The acquisition did add volume to the division, though, and Brannigan's customers eventually responded favorably, but the projected breakeven of two years turned into five.

Clark knew that Brannigan needed presence in these new flavors and the healthier soups the companies Claire identified offered. Acquisition seemed like an expedient way to obtain it. The acquisition prices seemed reasonable, but the issue of branding and marketing investment was complex. Clark felt that a minimum of 30% of sales would need to be spent for advertising and promotion if the acquired company's brand was continued. That percentage would have to continue for at least three years in order to grow the acquired line. The cost of advertising and promotion would be about half that number if the Brannigan's brand could be used instead of the acquired brand.

A plus was that the cost of the acquisition would be reflected in the balance sheet. Only interest and depreciation/amortization would affect operating income. Also, Brannigan's could provide manufacturing and operating synergies that should increase gross profit margins about 10% within two years. Clark knew the companies Mackey listed operated with about the same gross profit margins Brannigan's enjoyed in its core lines (45%) and their brands all commanded higher per unit selling prices than Brannigan's core products.

Cannibalization was a critical consideration. Clark felt Mackey's estimate was shy by half. Moreover, Brannigan faced a paradox from its retail partners. Most large retailers were trying to consolidate the number of vendors they dealt with, and from that perspective they would view Brannigan's purchasing a small company favorably. However, most retailers were wary of having their larger vendors, like Brannigan, gain shelf space. Clark knew that if a small company were acquired retailers would exert pressure on Brannigan to take out some of its weaker products so that Brannigan would have no net gain in shelf space after the acquisition. This same set of retailer concerns applied to new products.

If Brannigan's kept using the acquired brand name, the pressure from retailers to give up shelf space would be less, however. Clark estimated that maintaining the acquired brand, rather than changing to Brannigan's brand, would allow Brannigan to keep more than 90% of the acquired brand's shelf space, reducing cannibalization by 70% The marketing costs would be much higher, though, as outlined above. Against all these factors, Clark knew that the company was looking for a minimum of 10% ROI after five years of sales.

Bert moved on to the next email from his Chief Innovation Officer—the head of R&D.

Invest in organic growth from internally developed new products
From: chonga@brannigan.com
To: clarkb@brannigan.com

HI Bert

The soup report is dead on in highlighting consumer trends that we need to get in front of and lead rather than follow. Brannigan is a 100-year-old line with mature products in mature categories. Maybe we can get more boomers back to green bean and mushroom soup casseroles but it doesn't seem likely, given what we know about the market trends. That said, I sure hope we don't think the best way to grow is to buy another barking dog just because they have some snappy products that we could easily duplicate.

Here are my suggestions to reverse the market share and profit decline and move growth back to 3-4%:

- Milk our cash cows and invest in the rising stars. Srikant and I are in complete agreement that we should increase the advertising and promotional support for our new products. It is by far the most profitable way for us to go long term.
- Avoid thinking that we can short circuit the new product development process by just buying some small companies. Developing the products internally is far less expensive and ultimately much more profitable. Look at the struggle Srikant has had with the *Annabelle's Foods* products.
- Several new products are ready to launch that have tested well with consumers. I recommend increased spending for the new Ready-to-Eat (RTE) products from R&D including: "To-Your-Health

Chicken Noodle" and "Fast-and-Simple Mediterranean Tomato Basil." These reinforce our traditional strengths and strongly address consumers' changing needs.

- Up the R&D budget from $14 million to $19 million to increase the pace of new product creation and development. Here are several projects in development we feel have great potential:
  - Packaged "deli soups"
  - Simple Healthy "weight watchers" soups with a diet component
  - "Active Lifestyles" soups and broths
  - Convenient "Great Meals" related to, but different from, soups such as a dry or wet macaroni and cheese mix to be added to a pasta by the consumer.

These concepts squarely address the opportunities outlined in Julian's report and they could add significant growth and profit to our division. Here is an example of how I see the investment/return requirements to launch ten "typical" new products, ultimately ending up with one big new product winner (sales of more than 1% of the division's within two years):*

	$ in millions			
	2012*	2013	2014	2015
Development R&D	$2			
Marketing testing and launch		6		
On-going support			5	3
Net new volume		15	24	30
Incremental gross profit		7	12	16

* 2012 R&D budget of $14MM covers development of numerous products. Brannigan would likely have more than 100 in various stages of completion – conception, market research, testing, and launch. The $2MM shown is an "estimate" of development costs for 10 products. The other expenses shown are estimates for the same 10 products.

Please call to discuss. I hope we can move quickly to increase support for our vital new product development efforts.

Anna Chong, Chief Innovation Officer

Clark considered all the new product bombs he'd lived through during his career, along with the very low success rate for new products for the industry as a whole, outlined in the report. He thought Anna had some promising ideas, though, and the report did highlight consumer desire for innovation in the category. The new RTE flavors Anna proposed built on the most popular soups Brannigan offered and would permit a price increase of approximately $.10 a can. He thought this could result in an incremental net earnings increase of up to $12 million after spending 6% of the proposed advertising budget just for these specific new products, significantly more costly than shown in Chong's chart. Possibly, up to $6 million in additional gross profit might be achieved if additional shelf space could be obtained for the new products.

Clark felt that gaining shelf space for the new RTE products had about a 5% chance of occurring and was therefore very unlikely. But the profit gain from the price premium for the new RTE soups, even if all the sales were cannibalized (very likely if Brannigan has to take out core product to put in the new RTE soups) from Brannigan's core RTE soups, had a 90% chance of occurring.

As far as increasing R&D investment, he was wary of the continued optimism Anna and her team projected. Actually calculating new product investment returns was complicated by a number of factors. It was very hard to assign precise R&D costs to specific products that made it out of the lab to launch, as only a few did. Chong indicated that from about 100 ideas, ten new products were launched into the marketplace. This cost about $8MM per year as shown on the chart. Clark had reviewed data showing that of these ten new products, nine lasted in the market for less than two years. One of ten, though, would reach Brannigan's threshold for success outlined above ($30MM in sales two years from launch). Total profit from the sales from the nine new products that "failed" usually exceeded the amount invested in their development, however, even including the marketing expenses for them.

The larger "cost" to Brannigan concerned its retailers who were becoming increasingly intolerant of the cost to them of bringing in new products with short life-cycles that failed to meet their sales and profit expectations. Stocking fees, returns, and other charges that could be as much as a $1000 a store for *each* new product brought in and subsequently removed were a constant for Brannigan. And, Clark had no idea how to calculate the additional cost of the loss of retailers' goodwill.

Clark reached for the last email.

Invest in the core
From pughb@brannigan.com
To: clarkb@brannigan.com

Bert,

We've worked together a long time so I'll shoot straight.

I hope the report is a wake-up call. The Brannigan Soups core canned and RTE soups account for 64% of division sales and $210MM, or 71%, of the division's total profit. We have to act. I know the team doesn't necessarily see things my way, but we've been milking the core RTE wet soup lines to fund new products and acquisitions for the past five years. That strategy may have MBA logic behind it, but it's not working.

To keep profits up, our price increases on core products have been raised an average of 2% per year for the past five years. Now we're getting push-back from our major customers. Wal-Mart's private label soups have grown over 5% per year during the past five years while our shelf space in their stores has decreased by 3% there in that period. We can probably maintain a 15% to 20% price premium, but our 30%-higher pricing "gap" is just too large for consumers to ignore. At the same time, we've cut back advertising and promotion spending for our core products in order to meet the yearly profit goals.

These actions have resulted in a reduction in perceived "value" by our consumers and a diminution of the brand, a direct cause of our sales decline.

I signed off on this. The acquisition of *Annabelle*'s isn't living up to expectations, but it's not a disaster either. New products are another matter. The *Heart Healthy* line was a big investment and it has done little except to cannibalize our core products, as our market share continues to slide. We put these new products out there and the first thing our key retail partners ask us to do is take something out to make room for them on the shelf.

As many a parent has put it, "You need to dance with the one who brought you." We need to stop flirting with tiny companies and niche products and instead defend and fortify what the company has built over decades. Here are the actions I recommend. The time to implement them is now:

- Take a five cent price-per-can cut on the core ready-to-eat wet soups.[1]
- Increase the A&P budget by $20MM to restore fair share support for the brand.
- Bring back the Brannigan "Boys and Girls Love Soup" campaign to attract younger customers to the core RTE soups.
- Bring the manufacturing plants into the 21st century to rationalize what the price cuts will cost. Marcus (Operations Senior VP) indicated that would require about $22 million in capital.

---

[1] Wholesale cost per can of RTE soups was approximately $1.14 in 2011

- Let the sales force know in no uncertain terms that we're concentrating on growing the core Brannigan Soups as the number one goal this year.

With those actions, and assuming commodities prices are stable, operating income decline can be halted while we increase the sales volume and recapture market share. Here's my forecast:

(millions)		this year	next year
Cans of soup	RTE est	1,669	1800 - 2000
Advertising promotion		$189	$209

We've worked too hard over the past twelve years to let the big dog profit engine slip further.

Let's talk.

Bob Pugh, VP Sales and Marketing, Brannigan Soups

Clark thought Bob's view was shared by Brannigan's senior management and much of the sales force. He had serious reservations about cutting price, however. Retailers would favor it, of course, but would it really induce consumers to eat more soup from Brannigan?

Clark glanced at the rain outside and thought about the strong team he'd surrounded himself with. He reflected on their proposals and wondered whose ideas were most likely to provide the short-term numbers so desperately needed and which would strengthen the long-term direction of the company and its venerable brand.

He typed a few points onto his computer that needed to be clarified from each proposal: worst case, probable, best case.

He thought about the decision factors that might be pertinent and typed a quick list:

Volume vs. profit
Short term versus long term
Brand equity vs. Brand constraint
Category trend vs. performance
Health
Convenience
Risk of options
Opportunities and resource limits
What we do well
Competition

John Wilson was expecting a formal budget and action plan on his desk next week. The plan had to detail Clark's forecast for next year along with a three year overall sales and operating profit projection. Clark wondered how his forecast might change in light of his manager's proposals.

Exhibit 1 State of the Soup Industry: Summary Report

Julian J. DeGennaro, Brannigan Market Analyst, April 1, 2012

Soup Consumption in the US

The 2011 total of $6.4 billion sales in all categories (excluding Deli) represents a decline of 2.8% vs. 2010.

	2010	2011
Ready to serve wet soup	$2257M	$2020M
Condensed wet soup	1893	1821
Dry soup	1366	1397
Ready to serve broth	862	915
Refrigerated soups	142	164
Frozen soups	27	46
Deli soups	*110**	*140**

* Analyst's estimate, in addition to total market sales

Sales Drivers – Market Trends

- Continued sluggish economy will keep consumers eating at home and favor foods less than $2 per serving. A positive for soup.
- Soup continues to be perceived as a seasonal buy (67% sold November-March) with little innovation in the category.
- Concern over obesity, especially among children, and its health-related ramifications are likely to require manufacturers to stress healthy-living solutions
- Senior consumers (60+) are heavy consumers of soup and are brand loyal. This segment has growing health concerns and is looking for low sodium, fiber-enriched options. These products, however, are unappealing to younger consumer groups.
- High growth in "convenience" categories above are trend consistent with working moms
- Refrigerated and frozen soups are being branded by names associated with healthier fare like Panera Bread and Harry's Fresh Foods
- Supermarkets sold 62.9% of category

Soup Consumption by Household

- 1.4 cans, average consumed per week per US household
- Consumers, 18-24, average 2.1 cans per week, 48% eat dry soup
  78% eat wet soup
- High income consumers, 25-34, consume 40% of deli soups

Competition: US $6.4 Billion Soup Market

	Market Share	Brannigan's Ready to Eat (RTE)	
		Wet RTE	Condensed RTE
Brannigan's Foods	39.8 %	58.6	63.4
General Mills	24	15	12
Unilever	7	5	2
Other	13	3	1
Private Label	15.4	18	22

Market share data do not include "deli soups."

Premade "deli soup" poses a threat to packaged soup. 35% of respondents buy from supermarket deli sections. Consumers believe that deli soups are fresher and healthier. They clearly provide a "fast, simple" meal.

Consumer Information

38% of consumers eat as a snack millennials (age 15-30) with $25-49 income most likely to do so
91% of consumers agree that canned soup is good to keep in the pantry
55% say that they or someone in their household eats soup year round
86% are more likely to eat soup when the weather is cold
51% use soup as a cooking ingredient
78% agree that soup is a healthy/low calorie option   diet
61% of purchasers take low sodium into account when purchasing

Products

	New Products Introduced	(Industry Total)
	2010	2011
Wet Soup	236	217
Dry Soup	79	56

Benefit Claims: *In order of most used*

Microwavable
Ease of use
No additives or preservatives
All natural
Low fat

Flavors:

Southwest and Mexican hot and cold soups made up 11% of new products
Asian soups made up 8% of new products

Analyst's comments regarding new products

Brannigan's new product success rate of 7% parallels the general food industry. The low-sodium products introduced over the past five years now make up around 10% of the division's RTE soups, but have only allowed for some price increases. They have not increased soup consumption overall. These new items have not resulted in increased retail shelf space for Brannigan.

Brannigan's long effort to break into dry soups – most recently with a microwavable soft pouch package – has failed to pay back the $15MM investment in it.

Refrigerated and frozen soups are in channel locations that Brannigan has been unable to penetrate due to retailer reluctance to cede additional store space to the brand.

Strategic Challenges

Sales of Brannigan RTE Soups*	$ millions
Ready to Eat Condensed Soups	1080
Ready to Serve Wet Soup	1156

* Includes "Heart Healthy" low-sodium soups

Cream of Mushroom, Chicken Noodle, and Tomato are the most popular flavors in RTE Soups, selling 2.5 billion cans per year -- 41% of all soup sold.

Brannigan has 60% share of the RTE soup market; RTE soups and broths provide 78% of division's sales; 86% of its profits. Brannigan's RTE soups are mature products, in slow decline (1-2% per year in $s; 2-3% in volume)

Consumers perceive Brannigan to be behind competitors in the following:**

> Health trends
> Diet claims
> Convenience offerings
> Flavors – especially popular regional ones
> Seasonal products outside of cold weather

** 2010 Nielsen Survey

Retailers perceive Brannigan to be:

> The category leader in soups
> Not innovative
> Less profitable than store brands and competitors

Exhibit 2 Brannigan's Product Lines US Soups Division

	2012 sales ($ millions)
Traditional Ready to Eat (RTE) Soups	
Ready to serve wet soup	$ 998
Condensed wet soup	917
Broths	414
New products, acquisitions last ten years	
Tipha's lines	
Low sodium RTE " Heart Healthy"	321
Annabelle's Fast n Simple	71
Dry soups and mixes	53
Other, including private label	199
Total	2973

Exhibit 3 Clark's Preliminary Forecasts

Brannigan's Foods Consolidated Statement of Earnings US Soup Division

Year:	2011	2012est	2013 est
(in millions)			
Net Sales of Brannigan's Foods worldwide	7330	7979	8230
Net Sales of US Soup Division	3034	2973	2913
Less:			
Cost of goods sold	1669	1635	1602
Marketing, R&D and Selling Expense	425	416	408
Net Earnings	315	295	303
broken out of mktng and selling expense:			
Advertising & Promotion	189	178	170

Source: case writer, numbers above intended for classroom discussion only